THE EMERGENCE OF VOICE
IN LATINO/A HIGH SCHOOL STUDENTS

Studies in the Postmodern Theory of Education

Joe L. Kincheloe and Shirley R. Steinberg
General Editors

Vol. 147

PETER LANG
New York • Washington, D.C./Baltimore • Bern
Frankfurt am Main • Berlin • Brussels • Vienna • Oxford

ROSARIO DIAZ-GREENBERG

THE EMERGENCE OF VOICE IN LATINO/A HIGH SCHOOL STUDENTS

PETER LANG
New York • Washington, D.C./Baltimore • Bern
Frankfurt am Main • Berlin • Brussels • Vienna • Oxford

Library of Congress Cataloging-in-Publication Data

Diaz-Greenberg, Rosario.
The emergence of voice in Latino/a high school students / Rosario Diaz-Greenberg.
  p. cm. — (Counterpoints; vol. 147)
Includes bibliographical references and index.
1. Hispanic Americans—Education (Secondary)—Social aspects. 2. Hispanic American students—Social conditions. 3. Critical pedagogy—United States. I. Title. II. Counterpoints (New York, N.Y.); vol. 147.
  LC2670.4 .D53   373.1829'68073—dc21   99-089717
          ISBN 0-8204-4968-7
          ISSN 1058-1634

Die Deutsche Bibliothek-CIP-Einheitsaufnahme

Diaz-Greenberg, Rosario:
The emergence of voice in Latino/a high school students / Rosario Diaz-Greenberg.
−New York; Washington, D.C./Baltimore; Bern;
Frankfurt am Main; Berlin; Brussels; Vienna; Oxford: Lang.
(Counterpoints; Vol. 147)
ISBN 0-8204-4968-7

Cover design by Dutton & Sherman Design
Author photo by Silvia Esquivel

© 2003 Peter Lang Publishing, Inc., New York
275 Seventh Avenue, 28th Floor, New York, NY 10001
www.peterlangusa.com

All rights reserved.
Reprint or reproduction, even partially, in all forms such as microfilm, xerography, microfiche, microcard, and offset strictly prohibited.

Dedication

To the One and Only God, who is the center of my life,

To my parents,

My sisters,

My twins,

My teachers,

My students, and

My friends,

Your love, guidance, and support made this book possible

TABLE OF CONTENTS

List of Tables ix
Foreword xi
Acknowledgments..xxi
Introduction: A New Awareness: The Beginning of a Journey xxiii

- CHAPTER ONE
  The Structured Silence..1

- CHAPTER TWO
  Rupturing the Structured Silence..9

- CHAPTER THREE
  Eliciting Voices..37

- CHAPTER FOUR
  Emergent Themes and Emerging Voices.......................................55

- CHAPTER FIVE
  Reflections for the Future 81

References 93
Index..107

TABLES

- TABLE 1
  1981–1982 Principal's Annual Report
  on Ethnic Population 48

- TABLE 2
  1985–1986 Principal's Annual Report
  on Ethnic Population 48

- TABLE 3
  Comparision Chart of Ethnic Population
  Breakdown at E.H.S. 49

FOREWORD

I first met Professora Rosario Diaz-Greenberg at the California Association of Bilingual Education Conference in San Jose in 1996. With excitement and *ganas,* she was talking about *Clemencia, Pablo, Ruben, Alexia, Alicia, Ryan, Ana, Natalia, Yeiza, Anita, Danny, Guillermo, Madeleine, Lorraine, Rodrigo, Carolina, Sabrina,* and *Damisella*—teens you'll meet in this book (see *Chapter 3, Portraits of the Participants*). She said, "The organizing principle of [my teaching] rests on the premise that students are experts whose voices need to be elicited, validated, and heeded." Then she quoted Alicia, one of her students, who wrote (see Chapter 4 for details),

> The teachers at this school don't care about our culture. They do not incorporate culture in their classes. We have a lot to offer and most of this information comes from our parents, our families, but the teachers don't care about this.

She described Clemencia, who pleaded,

> Well, I wish education would not be so *automatizada.* The teachers have everything they need to teach in a teacher's guide book, even the tests, and they themselves and delve deeper [*profundizar*] in what is taught. They don't go any further than that. I believe the teachers should give more of themselves.

Listening to these teens express such deeply felt experiences of being rejected by their teachers and classmates because of their culture or their language, I felt a strong connection to the experiences of many children with disabilities who are rejected by their teachers and classmates, too. I heard the voices of the Latino/a teens and asked myself, "What would happen if the voices of children with disabilities could be heard this way? How would we teach differently if we treated children with disabilities as experts, too?" In other words, the teens' voices inspired me to learn more.

I would like to briefly state my qualifications in order to explain the context for my transformation. As professor of special education, I have devoted more than 30 years researching effective teaching and learning practices to accelerate the academic and social learning of students with special education needs. Currently I am a full professor at the College of Education faculty at Arizona State University West in Phoenix, Arizona, where I previously served as Coordinator of Undergraduate Teacher Education. In 2001, I was honored to be selected the scholar of the year at my university due, in part, to my productive career (for example, my research and teaching experiences have been published in more than 100 articles in refereed academic journals and I have co-authored 8 books). I have taught undergraduate and graduate education at major universities in California, Hawaii, Minnesota, and Indiana in addition to Vermont and Arizona. I have met a wide range of professors and learned diverse ways of thinking about education (e.g., direct instruction, reinforcement theory, creative thinking models, cooperative group learning, multiple intelligences models, computer assisted instruction, competency based or performance based assessment, self regulation and self determination skills training, collaborative consultation for special education teams, and so on).

Then, in 1997, while on sabbatical at Cal State San Marcos, Professora Diaz-Greenberg worked with me and other colleagues in the special education area (Dr. Jacqueline Thousand) as well colleagues from Arizona State University West such as Dr. Maria Cardelle-Elawar (educational psychology) and Dr. Carol Beckett (ESL teacher education) to study critical pedagogy. We began to ask, how might we apply the principles and concepts in our own teaching and research projects?

Professora Diaz-Greenberg invited me to attend her seminars to experience first hand her methods of teaching at the university. As our friendship grew, she insisted that I call her *"Rosario."* Because of our studies, I saw the potential for critical pedagogy and inclusive special education not only to form new relationships between teacher educators like ourselves, but new relationships for student teachers and their professors or student teachers and their own master teachers and students in the classroom. Rosario led me through a course of study that included Paulo Freire and Ira Shor. Their seminal work in transforming education effectively liberated people from the far distant farms of rural Brazil to the urban working class neighborhoods of Lower Manhattan. Their work is being refined by educators such as Alma Flor Ada and Antonio

Darder—people whom you will meet in Chapter 2. These notions came to life when my colleagues and I worked with Rosario to elicit and listen to the voices of adults with disabilities who spoke about their public school experiences.

I learned to introduce myself contextually, explaining more about who I am in relation to the familial as well as the socio-political contexts of my life. Now when I introduce myself when I'm speaking to my education students or at national or international conferences, I can say,

> I'm a participant-learner in this project to discover how critical pedagogy and inclusion might improve the education of children with disabilities. I am a female from a 2nd generation family of American Irish and Dutch descent. I've been fortunate to be born into a *zeitgeist* and family culture where education for girls was valued as a way to give to the world as well as a way to improve oneself and the family. I'm a sister to 4 siblings, a life-long learner, a teacher/scholar, a mother, an aunt, a wife, a grandmother, a friend, a mentor, an international traveler. The strengths I bring to whatever I do include 30 years of working with many people to help students with disabilities succeed.

Doesn't this sound more personal and informative than the previous paragraph listing my accomplishments? I've discovered that many audiences prefer this method of meeting me.

Through Rosario's writing,[1] I met "Sonya." Rosario teaches her education students using a critical pedagogy action research process to transform reality by following a 4 stage problem-posing approach espoused by Paolo Freire[2]—questioning, reflecting, voicing, and taking action. In her Methods and Theories of Bilingual Education class (required for all bilingual secondary candidates), her preservice teachers use the critical action research model to determine a specific issue that puzzles them in their internship classrooms, reflect on the causes that might influence such an issue, voice their concerns to the class, and proceed to take action. The process is self-empowering and provides a forum for individual and collective action.

Sonya wanted to determine the qualities of a good English as a Second Language (ESL) teacher as perceived by high school native Spanish speakers. Her research design put the students' voices at the center, validated their input, legitimized the shift in power relationships

---

[1] Keating, Joseph, Diaz-Greenberg, Rosario, Baldwin, M., & Thousand, Jacqueline. (1998). A collaborative action research model for teacher preparation programs. *Journal of Teacher Education, 49*(3), 381-390.

[2] Freire, Paolo. (1970). *Pedagogy of the oppressed.* NY: Seabury.

between teacher and students as researchers. Sonya's first step was to identify a compelling question: What are the characteristics of a good ESL teacher from the point of view of native Spanish speakers? Sonya sought input from other interns in her class, as well as professors, to design a questionnaire with five open ended questions that she distributed to a total of 130 Latino/a high school students in the two schools where she interned. This provided a naturally occurring comparison group.

Sonya interviewed her classmates and professors in the process of designing her questionnaire. After reviewing the questionnaires, she found 33 were non-native speakers of Spanish. She selected the remaining 97 to analyze because her focus was the perceptions of native Spanish speakers. She looked for generative themes (Freire, 1970) and found 3 major themes: personal qualities, methodological approaches, and positive reinforcement. Sonya encouraged students to write in both English and Spanish, which she could translate.

Theme #1: The personal qualities most often mentioned were nice, friendly, sympathetic, enthusiastic, helpful, "carinosa/o" (affable/loving), and patient. Most comments referred to the quality of patience such as,

> She took the time to explain.

> He went to great lengths to make sure we understood.

> She didn't get mad if we asked the same question.

> She showed us her humanness.

Theme #2: The teaching techniques that accommodated their learning styles were appreciated.

> She used drawings to explain words.

> She told us stories and then let us talk about them.

Theme #3: Positive reinforcement was the most valued aspect to the high school students. They appreciated encouragement, compassion, prodding, and gentle pushing.

> She wants us to learn.

> She makes us learn.

> She gives us ganas (desire) to learn. She thinks we can learn.

In conducting the yearlong critical pedagogy action research project, Sonya was able to use her direct experience to corroborate many principles and theories she had learned in Professora Diaz-Greenberg's class. In Sonya's words,

> ESL teachers [who] provide drawings and explanations, along with positive reinforcement, comfortable non-threatening environments, with a caring attitude seemed to motivate students.

Sonya concluded her report with the following suggestions to help future ESL teachers become effective agents of change in their communities.

> [Developing] Confidence in speaking through self esteem building and acknowledging that each learner has individual learning needs are the qualities of a 'good' English teacher. Each student brings her own issues, be they social, behavioral, or academic to school. The 'good' English teacher must be able to see each student as an individual and give each student the self-esteem and *ganas* (desire) to continue their language development. A 'good' English teacher cares about the success of students.

Sonya's research as an intern-student teacher is one reason why I am such a strong advocate of a critical pedagogy approach. I have seen it work wonders in such diverse areas. Sonya's authentic teacher-researcher voice rings as true to me as the voice of published professors. In fact, although I've never met her, Sonya's voice inspired me to apply her advice to my own teaching. I have since learned to more consciously and conscientiously model sheltered English techniques so that my own special education student teachers can meet the needs of dual language learners with disabilities.

Rosario's successes as a teacher whose students learned to apply a critical pedagogy approach to their own research questions inspired me to teach a critical pedagogy approach with my own graduate students at Arizona State University West while we were struggling to apply concepts of collaborative consultation to work with new audiences in early childhood special education. The California Consortium of Critical Educators is another source of constant feedback about the successes. Through conferences, email, and sharing of articles, I hear about critical situations where others are eliciting and taking action based on the voices of people with diverse views and needs.

I am a much better teacher and researcher as a consequence of a critical pedagogy approach. I no longer judge my students as wrong or contrary for the way they might express themselves. In fact, I have learned to welcome their voices and use the information to help liberate them and myself from our previously held beliefs. This helps all of us move forward to new ways of thinking and behaving with people who have seemingly contrary views to ours. I've learned to ask questions and listen in new ways to help all of us develop new stories and examples to speak to the hearts and minds of our various audiences.

But perhaps more important, I have become even more committed to taking action to correct social injustices. I am now a member of an international advocacy organization and sit on a statewide advisory council where others with similar commitments do more than talk about change and instead take meaningful (but sometimes very small) steps to make changes. This is how critical pedagogy has changed my life. And it all began because I heard *Clemencia, Pablo, Ruben, Alexia, Alicia, Ryan, Ana, Natalia, Yeiza, Anita, Danny, Guillermo, Madeleine, Lorraine, Rodrigo, Carolina, Sabrina,* and *Damisella*—the Latino/a teens you'll meet in this book.

Be aware there is one barrier you may encounter as you listen to their voices. It is often very difficult to realize that they are speaking about things we wish did not exist. As a teacher myself, I deeply regret that these young souls have had to experience rejection and ridicule, humiliation and silencing, at the hands of people in my chosen profession. I worry that I, too, might inadvertently (surely not consciously) perpetuate similar suppression of my own students' unique individualities. I have come to appreciate that one of my responsibilities is to stop living an unexamined life—that I must listen to what others are saying in order to discover my own biases and prejudices. Yes, it is very difficult to unlearn what I have previously supposed to be true.

Just one example from modern special education might help put this into perspective. One of my personal heroes in special education has been Bruno Bettelheim, a pioneer in the treatment of children with autism. However, he refused to receive new information about the sources of autism, believing until his death that it was caused by the child's failure to bond with a nurturative mother. Recent advances in medicine have determined that autism is more like cerebral palsy, a neurological condition—a movement difference—rather than an emotional disorder. You can imagine how differently teachers might interact with a child with a movement difference—compared to how they might teach a child with an emotional difference. How can we set aside our passionately held beliefs, especially those that are well researched and have a strong database? That is the promise of a liberatory critical pedagogy approach to teaching.

Foreword

In fact, due to Rosario Diaz-Greenberg, seminal study of Latino/a voices and her willingness to coach her colleagues, the voices of those with disabilities have become a powerful source of inspiration for changing my own beliefs. As we listened to more and more voices of people with disabilities, my colleagues and I developed a series of teacher actions that help special educators teach for liberation (Kluth, Diaz-Greenberg, Thousand, and Nevin, 2002[3]). Listen to Gena,[4] a 19-year old Norwegian Irish-American who attended a university secondary teacher education program majoring in English. At 15, Gena was diagnosed as having bipolar disorder.

> "First I was diagnosed with just basic depression. Then I was diagnosed with bipolar, and then I was diagnosed with alcoholism and drug addiction. They put me on loads of medication, Prozac and Lithium. Looking back, it's the most detrimental thing you can do to a person because you are teaching them that numbness is the solution." She explained, "I value honesty and being true to myself. I am a person who questions, I don't know if authority is the right word, but just questions things.... "[In high school], "I made certain cries for help that were quite large. I was not fooling around. I gave my suicide note to my English teacher, and she just said, 'Why did you give this to me? I think [my] teachers had a habit of ignoring my voice or voices in general. But I don't think school has shown me who I am. I guess a big thing that school did for me is it showed me that I want to be a teacher, because when I have real bad teachers, I don't want to be like them. I don't want to talk down to kids. The same as when I have excellent teachers, I see qualities [in them] that I want to have."

Through our research efforts, we met Dr. Paula Kluth, a Syracuse University researcher who applied Paulo Freire's critical pedagogy principles to listen to the voices of students who used facilitative communication. One of her students, Candy[5], was diagnosed with *microcephaly*; she doesn't speak and when she was 16, her individual

---

[3] Kluth, P., Diaz-Greenberg, R., Thousand, J., & Nevin, A. (2002 Teaching for Liberation. In J. S. Thousand, R. A. Villa, & A. I. Nevin (Eds.). *Creativity and collaborative learning: The practical guide to empowering students, teachers, and families*, 2nd Ed., (p. 71-83). Baltimore, MD: Paul H. Brookes Publishing Co.

[4] From Diaz-Greenberg, R., Thousand, J., Beckett, C., Cardelle-Elawar, M., Nevin, A., & Reese, R. (1999, February). *Critical pedagogy and inclusion: Common struggles for change as expressed by voices from the field*. Paper presented at the meeting of the California Bilingual Education 99, Los Angeles.

[5] Kluth, P. (1998). The impact of facilitated communication on the educational lives of students: Three case studies. Doctoral dissertation. Madison, WI: University of Wisconsin-Madison, Special Education Department.

education program indicated that her 'severe cognitive disabilities' prevented her from "adequate learning at a high school curriculum level." However, just a few months later, after she learned to use facilitated communication, her diagnosis was changed to mild mental retardation and she was allowed to attend the same school as her sisters. Candy began to express her need to be seen as an intelligent person. She relished the opportunity to have a more personal and interactive experience with a psychology professional because her previous experiences with psychologists involved assessments of her intelligence and other measurements of her disability. She wanted others to talk to her "like they do to each other." Candy typed over and over again, "Want friends, need friends."

Thanks to the explicit step-by-step process described in this book (see Chapter 3), the voices of teachers as well as their students are now being heard. I believe that the dialogic retrospection process that Rosario used—interviewing, giving feedback to the interviewee, and re-interviewing—can become a powerful process for eliciting ideas for how to change our educational system by changing our words, actions, character, and thus, our destiny.

I have become enheartened by the preliminary results of this dialogic dialectic process to elicit voice. As a caution, I am reminded that those who practice both a critical pedagogy approach and an inclusive education approach must be self-conscious about the process of re-inventing. "Freire never wished his 'method' to be a method. He loathed the idea of his approach being replicated, so he constantly cautioned us against it." (Rosario Diaz-Greenberg, e-mail communication to the Critical Pedagogy and Inclusion research team, 7/8/99.) Whereas it is true that some of the groups that Freire worked with held certain commonalities, the most important issue was to let each individual realize the power of her individuality and then look at what could be done to change her and the group's reality. This is where critical pedagogy and the inclusion movement touch each other. The most important principle from both critical pedagogy and the inclusion movement lies in this suggestion for action, creating a new world.

I wanted further dialogue about the unique perspectives that critical pedagogy and inclusion might bring to creating a context for mutual change, support, and social justice. The goal was to achieve the vision of inclusive education for people with disabilities from all cultures. At a 3-day institute, Rosario and I were joined by critical pedagogists from

Chapman University and special education colleagues from Cal State San Marcos. We posed a series of questions to special educators who attended the international TASH conference in 2001.

As a result of the dialogues with over 50 interested teacher educators, educators, advocates, and people with disabilities, several actions were proposed to help special educators become liberatory educators. Teachers can break the culture of silence by encouraging their students to interview each other and family members and discover basic information about their countries of origin, their special needs, their customs. Teachers can shift the power relationships in their classrooms by simply engaging in new actions such as teaching children to question what the teacher is saying, changing who evaluates assignments, co-constructing classroom rules of conduct. Teachers can use new collaborative pedagogy such as critical literacy and coaching or mentoring their students. Teachers can teach for liberation by changing the pace of a dialogue to give more time to think before providing answers. They can create space for sharing in the daily classroom routine. They can listen in new ways. Franklin,[6] for example, is a teenager, now a college student, with movement challenges who advises teachers to "listen with your whole body."

And, by taking new actions outside the classroom, teachers can enjoy the outcomes of Paulo Freire's principle of *praxis*, reflecting then acting on the basis of new understandings. For example, teachers can engage in political movements to change the ways in which children are treated in schools. Working within the school curriculum committee structures, teachers can advocate replacing punitive disciplinary systems with proactive social skills programs that can often do more to help students deal positively with bullying and teasing, actions that often take place outside of teachers' domains. The Latino/a teens you'll meet in this book also realized new ways of acting after they had reflected on their new understandings about culture and language and their schooling experiences. Listen to Alexia who achieved what Cross[7] described as

---

[6] Kluth, P. (1999, Dec.). Developing successful schooling experiences for FC users: An interview with Franklin and Pat Wilson. Facilitative Communication Institute Newsletter, 8(1), 7–11. Available on the World Wide Web: http://soeweb.syr.edu/thefci/7-2klu.htm

[7] Cross, W. (1978). The Thomas and Cross models of psychological nigrescence: A literature review. *Journal of Black Psychology*, 4, 13–31.

internalization, a stage of identity which is characterized by "a calm, secure demeanor [where] ideological flexibility, psychological openness, and self-confidence...are evident." Can you detect what Alexia plans to do about passing on her way of life?

> I have always been aware of my Latin American heritage, but before, when I lived in my country, I did not appreciate it as much and took it for granted. Now that I live in the United States I am very proud of everything related to my culture and I do not regret being a Latina.
>
> My life has changed due to the fact that now I am prouder of my heritage and feel good when I speak about it, so that I can educate others and help them understand the Latino way of life. Now I appreciate more the cultural traditions of my country. To me, culture signifies my customs, my roots, my traditions, my way of life. Culture is a very important part of my life because it reflects my way of life and it is something I want to pass on to my children and grandchildren in the future.

In Chapters 4 and 5, you will discover more about Alexia's beliefs as well as what happened to the other teens, *Clemencia, Pablo, Ruben, Alicia, Ryan, Ana, Natalia, Yeiza, Anita, Danny, Guillermo, Madeleine, Lorraine, Rodrigo, Carolina, Sabrina, and Damisella.*

By now, perhaps, you can see that you receive a three-fold gift in this book. First, you can be assured that the principles and practices used to elicit voices of Latino/a teens are based on sound educational research. Second, Rosario's teaching tactics come to life. You will read how she elicits, validates, and acts upon the voices of the students in her classrooms. Third, and perhaps most importantly, the teens themselves come to life. Their experiences have the potential to possibly change forever your life, the lives of those you teach, and the lives of those you love.

May your own journey to new thoughts and new actions be as joy-filled and challenging as mine has been. In closing, I sincerely thank my friend and *colega*, Professora Rosario Diaz-Greenberg, for her decision to write this book. By doing so, she shows her values for listening to her students and taking actions to help them succeed.

Ann I. Nevin, Ph. D., Professor
Phoenix, Arizona

ACKNOWLEDGMENTS

The completion of this book represents, to me, finally coming to voice by rupturing the structured silence of domination and oppression often experienced by Latinos in the educational system. It means the beginning of another stage in my struggle to promote social justice and equality. During this process I have grown intellectually, emotionally, and spiritually. Also, I have been able to strengthen my own beliefs and re-conceptualize the true meaning of praxis. Having the opportunity to become more aware of the multiple realities and struggles forever present in the lives of Latino students has increased my lifelong commitment to multilingual/multicultural education.

Many individuals have played an important role in the development of this book. I wish to acknowledge my editors, Joe Kinchloe and Shirley Steinberg, my dear friend and mentor, Ann Nevin, my longtime companion in struggle, Catherine Walsh, from whom I learned the true meaning of praxis, my teachers, Alma Flor Ada, Dennis Collins, Sr. Mary Peter Traviss, Antonia Darder, and Maria Torres Guzman. They believed in me and provided me the support I needed during each stage of my writing.

A special acknowledgment is extended to my friends, Jacque Thousand, Lettie Ramirez, Olivia Gallardo, Duarte Silva, Rosalia Salinas, Bea Gonzalez, and Lupe Buell, for always being there when I needed them.

Above all I want to thank the members of my immediate and extended family in the United States, Mexico, and El Salvador. Without their constant support and understanding I would have never completed this book.

INTRODUCTION
A New Awareness:
The Beginning of a Journey

My journey began many years ago as I came from El Salvador to the United States to learn English as a Second Language. I now realize that this journey will never end for, as a life-long learner, I will continue to learn for as long as I live. I have embraced this process with trepidation yet I am fully aware of the actions I need to take. I want to remember how it all began and how my own *conscientization* process evolves. As I write I weep, not just for who I was, but for who I have become. I cannot regress in time, but I can regain what I have lost: my voice, my identity, and a part of my own self.

I was born and raised in San Salvador, the capital of El Salvador, where I attended an all-girls Catholic private school until I graduated from high school. At the age of seventeen I was sent to Boston, MA to learn English as a Second Language. A year later I moved to New York City, where I attended Marymount Manhattan College and, later on, Hunter College. I was fortunate to work for the United Nations as a bilingual guide while going to school. Such work opened my eyes to the need of making changes at the grassroots level. Thus, I changed my career from the Diplomatic Corp to becoming a bilingual teacher for the City of New York.

After teaching in several inner-city schools in New York City I was able to return to El Salvador and began teaching at the American School. Unfortunately, the Civil War in El Salvador ensued four years later, and I had to return to Florida, where I taught for the next fourteen years.

I began my doctoral studies at the University of San Francisco when I was still teaching high school in Florida. Having to commute across the country every other weekend was very difficult. In the end my family and I moved to California, where I taught in an inner-city school for a year and then became an assistant professor of education at California State University San Marcos.

The world of academia is full of challenges for everyone, especially people of color. Often times our cultural views clash with the culture of the school, creating difficult situations, which can lead us to give up our identities and silence our voices. Staying true to my own beliefs has been one of the most important challenges in academia, and it has caused me to reflect on my role as a woman of color.

I am now an Associate Professor with Tenure and have spent my sabbatical helping redesign the national curricula for schools in El Salvador. My passion for social justice and equality, my ability to love, and my trust in God continue to sustain me in the struggle. I know now that I must go on for as long as I live, for there are others following in my footsteps. However small my contribution is, I want to make a difference in their lives.

On Becoming a Critical Educator

During my years as a doctoral student I was able to reflect on who I was as a human being. Such processes helped me to crystallize my views on education and opened my eyes to another world. The realization that I too belonged to the dominant group by holding the values instilled in me by my teachers and my colleagues did not come easily.

For a long time I had tried to define who I was and what was my place in society. By involving myself in professional and social activities I felt that I was already doing my part to help others. However, it was not until I began to examine myself in terms of my culture and ethnicity that I truly saw who I was. It was difficult to admit that there were many aspects of myself which I had to explore. Being forced to examine and explain who I am to others made me reflect and revisit my past through dialogic retrospection, which is one aspect of Critical Pedagogy.

Dialogic Retrospection

Dialogic retrospection is a powerful process leading both to the dialogue with others and to the dialogue with oneself. This internal dialogue may provide the space for awakening the self, reclaiming the inner voice, and arriving at the realization that one is capable of promoting change.

Introduction: A New Awareness: The Beginning of a Journey

The awakening of the self is perhaps one of the most painful aspects of this process. It involves the realization that, for years, one has been a victim of internalized oppression. This realization, though illuminating, evokes memories that have been suppressed for a long time. As a result, reflection takes the form of revisiting the past.

I faced a lot of inner turmoil as I examined my past and re-examined the values that I held. I felt a lot of sorrow as I shed tears for the person that I was and the person that I wanted to be.

I realized that it was from my schoolteachers that I had acquired most of my values. Their vision of *Kultur* was based on canons and societal norms which discarded anything that did not conform to such beliefs. This view of Kultur permeated my own reality. For years I was molded to conform to my teachers' views of society, thereby becoming a member of the dominant class and exercising what I considered my own rights. Despite my father's efforts to show me what my people's *culture* was, I grew up to adopt a distorted view of the society and culture that I lived in.

As the years went by I continued to acquire what I now realize was a distorted view of the world around me. The saddest part was that I accepted my reality as being unchangeable. And I felt the helplessness of what I thought was a pre-set course for my life.

In revisiting the past, I was forced to reevaluate the actions I had taken even with the period of anguish that followed. In turn, I discovered that this anguish was dissipated by the realization that any action taken in the past is no longer what really counts. In fact I learned that each action is a continuation of another, and it only represents a single step in the road of life.

When I reclaimed my inner voice I experienced joy. Reclaiming my inner voice meant that I now had the ability to frame, with words, the feelings that have been awakened within my inner self. As such, reclaiming my voice does not only mean being able to phrase one's own feelings, it also means the reclaiming of an identity, a personal name, or one's own cultural heritage. In my case, it meant no longer being called Rose, an Americanized version of my name, and instead being called Rosario, which is my full Spanish name.

The mere fact that an individual can, at this point, become proud of who she/he actually is reflects the empowering impact that dialogic retrospection can have. As an individual reclaims this inner voice, she/he also reclaims the voices of those people she/he encounters. This became evident as my own students began to echo my discoveries in their own way: For example, Lina, a Latina high school student who I taught, wrote:

> In this class we learn about ourselves, our culture, our roots...we become proud of who we are.

The realization that one is capable of promoting change is, perhaps, the most powerful and yet, the most frightening aspect of this process. It is powerful because one becomes aware of the fact that the circumstances around one's own life do not have to dictate one's own course for action. It is frightening because, as one begins to take action, the consequences that such action might cause become very evident.

Each action is then taken under the full realization that its consequences might not cause the joy, pleasure, or recognition that one is accustomed to expect. When I teach, my students no longer make piñatas and paper flowers which in the past had been used to decorate the library and hallways as a way to honor my culture. Instead, I engage in dialogue by encouraging my students to do participatory research projects on topics which are relevant to my students' own realities, such as racism and discrimination against Latinos in the school setting. Consequently, colleagues begin to question what is happening in my classes and why I no longer want to go along with the activities that had brought recognition and accolades to the department in the past.

Dialogic retrospection is also a humbling experience. It makes a person become aware of her/his own limitations. In a way, it forces an individual to trust the process without fear. Yet, as human nature dictates, trusting the process is not easy for many individuals. My realization that there is no end to the road and that each action is just a step within the process helps me to continue in spite of my fears.

Personally I have had a difficult time letting go and blindly trusting the process. Always knowing what to expect was part of my approach to life. As I entered this process I thought I knew who I was. However, after several weeks I realized that I had a lot of searching to do. The feelings of shame triggered a desire to take action and truly try to begin defining my own self.

Engaging in dialogical retrospection has allowed me to become, as one of my mentors, Alma Flor Ada (1990a), promised,

> ...more full of compassion, more generous, more willing to provide, to give, to challenge myself...to Become...to be empowered to develop [my] best

resources as a human being [and my own] possibilities of growth. (Ada, 1990a, p. 4)

As I reflect on the personal transformation that has taken place within me, I realize that I have only begun to tap the reservoir of my inner self. It is as if each day I become aware of many new facets that I never knew existed within me. This is frightening because I do not know where it will all lead me. Yet, I realize that there is no turning back. I am also aware of the fact that, as I transform, my family and my students transform with me. On one side, I am glad to be able to lead myself, my family, and my students to new realms of "*concientizacion.*" On the other side, I worry about what the consequences might be. Again I need to state that it is with trepidation that I now *embrace* this process.

Seeing my students transform has been the most rewarding aspect of this part of the process. Their personal reflections and the trust that they have placed in me represent the commitment that I have made to the betterment of society. I am grateful for the opportunity to learn from others. However, I sometimes wonder, if I had known ahead of time how difficult it would be, would I have embarked in this journey to reclaim my voice. It is very hard to feel a part of a community where others are not yet acquainted with Critical Pedagogy. This means that sometimes I feel that my voice is not heard. At the same time, I am thankful that I have the courage to continue to express my voice with my students and colleagues, many of whom I now consider my extended family.

CHAPTER ONE
The Structured Silence

The subordination, suppression, and silencing of bilingual students' voices and their communities by the educational system has come under scrutiny during the past decade (Darder, 1991; Poplin, 1991b; Walsh, 1991a). This study seeks to provide a forum for students' voices by examining some of the factors that promote the silencing of voice in Latino high school students and submerse them in the culture of silence (Freire, 1985; Shor & Freire, 1987). It explores how students perceive their cultural and linguistic reality, their family history, and their home experiences within the educational system. It also looks at what students foresee as alternatives for promoting educational reform, aiding the emergence and legitimization of their voices, and attempting to deconstruct practices that tend to encode privilege, power, and marginality in the public school system. Perhaps when the educational system listens to students' voices it will become a democratic sphere, thus opening up the encoded structure of silences often imposed on the less privileged (Weis & Fine, 1993).

During the past two decades, the deplorable economic, physical, intellectual, and moral conditions that exist within the public schools have caused an outcry for reform (Boyer, 1987; Goodlad, 1984; Kozol, 1991; McLaren, 1989; Poplin and Weeres, 1992; Silberman, 1970; Sizer, 1984). Among the most affected by adverse conditions in the educational system are bilingual children, who constitute a statistically significant and increasingly large percentage of the public schools' population. According to the 1990 U.S. Census, 31.8 million—one out of every seven—persons in the United States speak a language other than English at home. The majority of these people, whose numbers have increased from 11.1 million in 1980 to 17.3 million in 1990, speak Spanish:

> Reflecting the youth of the Spanish-speaking population in comparison with many other language groups, Spanish speakers are a larger proportion of the school-age HSNELS [home speakers of non-English language] populations

than of the adult population.... In 1990, they constituted two-thirds of the five-to-seventeen-year-olds but only a little more than half of the adults. The growth in the number of Spanish speakers accounts for nearly 70 percent of the growth in school-age HSNELS population. (Waggoner, 1993, p. 6)

In the year 2000 the majority of students in public schools are children of color with approximately 80% of them being Latino (Trueba, 1989).

The education provided to bilingual children in general, and Latino students in particular, "is tied to a complex series of historical, sociocultural, and political relations, concerns, and conditions...which include issues of race, class, colonialism, and power" (Walsh, 1992). Such issues include the interaction between schools and families, the underlying effort toward assimilation of children of color into mainstream American society, and the imposition of a non-inclusive traditional curriculum that enhances the values and traditions of Western civilization. Latino children experience a higher dropout rate than any other group (Walsh, 1991a), and, by the age of 17, many of them are classified as functionally illiterate (Fueyo, 1988).

The interaction between schools and families who come from diverse ethnic and linguistic backgrounds has been the subject of research for many scholars (Ada, 1988b; Bronfenbrenner, 1986; Cazden, Carrasco, Maldonado-Guzman & Erickson, 1985; Cochran & Dean, 1991; Delgado-Gaitan, 1992; Harry, 1992; Jordan & Au, 1981; Ogbu, 1982; Phillips, 1983; Siegel & Laosa, 1983; Soto, 1989, 1992; Trueba, 1989; Wong Fillmore, 1990). Some educators in the United States still underestimate the contributions of Latino families and attribute the underachievement of Latino students to the inferiority of their culture, the organization of their family values, and a lack of interest in education (Dunn, 1987). Latino families are given the status of a minority and their contributions to the educational system are not considered valuable (Diaz-Soto, 1993). A similar concern was illustrated by Ada (1990a), who claimed that often the educational system does not recognize or value the culture, language, and home-based experiences of children of color.

An underlying effort to make all students assimilate into what is considered the American mold implies that the children of newly arrived immigrants should adapt to the language and customs of mainstream society in North America (Fitzgerald, 1993). As a result, Latino students are asked to deny their origins and adopt a cultural heritage that is not theirs. The assimilation of American values and standards and the abandonment of cultural and ethnic heritage is expected of children of color in order for them to become "good" U.S. citizens (Darder, 1992). Frantz Fanon described a comparable case referring to the situation of black people from the Antilles: "The Negro of the Antilles will be proportionately whiter—that is, he will come closer to being a real human being—in direct ratio to his mastery of the French language" (1967, p. 18).

Educational institutions usually follow a traditional curriculum, and high school certification depends on the completion of a certain number of courses. Such courses stress the attitudes and values of the dominant society and have as common principles the reproduction of a set of canons that are monolithic and non-inclusive. By perpetuating the values and social stratification existent in American society, education promotes the reproduction and legitimization of the worldview of the dominant majority, thus ignoring the perspectives of people of color (Darder, 1992). Aronowitz and Giroux (1985) expressed a parallel view:

> The dominant school culture functions not only to legitimate the interests and values of dominant groups; it also functions to marginalize and disconfirm knowledge forms and experiences that are extremely important to subordinate and oppressed groups. This can be seen in the way in which school curricula often ignore the histories of women, racial minorities, and the working class.... Schools legitimate dominant forms of culture through the hierarchically arranged bodies of knowledge that make up the curriculum as well as the way in which certain forms of linguistic capital and the individual (rather than collective) appropriation of knowledge is rewarded in schools. (pp. 147–148)

Fanon (1967) contended that the oppressor, by distorting, disfiguring, and destroying the past, contributes to the annihilation of identity in the oppressed. Latino children, believing that their past history and culture do not exist as a part of the school curriculum, embrace a different culture, that of the dominant society, in order to blend in. Octavio Paz defined this situation as "el ninguneo," which means to pretend mentally that one does not exist in relationship to one's own culture and ethnicity on the outside world. As a result, the development of the secret "other," which Paz said "could only be met in the secret of the darkness" (1962, p. 14), or among those who share the same cultural background and ethnicity, takes place. Ada (1990a) explained that by emulating the behavior of the majority and shedding their language, identity, and names, children of color hope to be accepted as members of the dominant society, which often results in the development of a different personality. All these factors contribute to the success or failure experienced by Latino students as they struggle to reclaim their voices and become agents of effective change in society.

> The concept of voice spans literal, metaphorical, and political terrains: In its literal sense, voice represents the speech and perspectives of the speaker; metaphorically, voice spans inflection, tone, accent, style and the qualities and feelings conveyed by the speaker's words; and politically, a commitment to voice attests to the right of speaking and being represented. (Britzman, 1989, p. 146)

The purpose of this study is to explore through students' reflections some of the factors that lead to the silencing of voice in Latino high school students in the United States and what happens when their voices emerge. The purpose is also to discover how students perceive their own cultural and linguistic reality within the classroom, and to explore some alternatives that can promote the emergence and legitimization of voice in the American educational system. This study aims to listen to the silent voices of students and learn from them by accepting their words as an untapped and rich source of thoughts and feelings that can serve to create knowledge for teachers and students (Shor, 1992).

Based on Freire's concept of "conscientizacao" and his "culture of silence," the theoretical framework of this study addresses the voicelessness often experienced by Latino individuals in the high school system. Within the culture of silence, "the masses are mute, that is, they are prohibited from creatively taking part in the transformation of their society and therefore prohibited from being" (1985, p. 50). As a result, individuals are rendered voiceless by a system that is controlled by those in power:

> The dependent society is by definition a silent society. Its voice is not an authentic voice, but merely an echo. Only when the people of a dependent society break out of the culture of silence and win their right to speak—only, that is, when radical structural changes transform the dependent society—can such a society as a whole cease to be silent toward the director society. (Freire, 1985, p. 73)

According to Goulet (1992), in the United States, oppression is expressed in multiple forms. Thus, there exists a specific garb that is worn by and characterizes those members of society who are a part of the culture of silence, and that can only be identified by those individuals who have been historically submersed in it. Led to believe that their lives are condemned to a cycle of poverty and violence, millions of Latino students in America experience a similar situation.

Freire's epistemology (1985), evolving from his work in Third World countries and contained in his early writings, *Pedagogy of the Oppressed* (1970) and *Education for Critical Consciousness* (1973), aims to promote the liberation of the self by asking individuals to name their world, reflect upon their reality, and act to transform it. In the United States, Freire's theories have provided the basis for a transformative approach to education as demonstrated by the works of Ada (1992, 1990a, 1990b, 1988a, 1988b), Auerbach & Wallerstein (1987), Apple & King (1977), Aronowitz & Giroux (1991, 1985), Darder (1995, 1992, 1991), Fine (1987), Giroux (1991, 1989, 1988, 1983), McLaren (1989), Poplin (1993, 1991a, 1991b, 1991c), Shor (1992), and Walsh (1996, 1994, 1993, 1991a, 1991b), among others.

This study aims to answer the following questions:

1. What are some of the factors that lead to the silencing of voice in Latino high school students?
2. What happens when their voices emerge?
3. What do students perceive as their cultural and linguistic reality within the educational system?
4. What are some alternatives that can promote the emergence and legitimization of voice in the educational system?

This study provides a forum for the expression of students' voices. The literature on the subject of students' voices is increasing. Most of what exists has been written from a theoretical perspective; studies that actually incorporate students' voices are only beginning to emerge (Brown, 1993; LeBoeuf 1990; Mercado, 1993; Nieto 1994; Poplin and Weeres, 1992; Shaw, 1993; Walsh, 1996, 1991a; Wu, 1990; Zanger, 1994). The significance of this study rests on three assumptions: (1) its ability to draw out, explore, and document how Latino students perceive their cultural and linguistic reality; (2) its presentation of curricular and methodological approaches and alternatives to promote the emergence and legitimization of students' voices; and (3) its insight into and revelation of the ways shared teacher/student experiences, language, and culture can shape as well as impact both classroom relations and the emergence of voice.

> Those pushed to the margins are struggling for voice at the same time as those with privilege are gathering their energies to call for exclusive hegemonic

> voice. This "chorus of difference" now litters our schools, but it could be so much more thoughtfully incorporated into the educational life of schooling. We wish to encourage attention to these voices, ever mindful and delighted that they flourish both in harmony and in conflict. (Weis & Fine, 1993, p. 6)

There are several delimitations that need to be taken into consideration. First, this study covers a span in the lives of adolescents marked by a presupposed growth in maturation. Second, it focuses on words, reflections, and perspectives that emanate from a particular group of students' lives. Relevant to and reflective of their own lived experiences, as well as the manner and context in which the words were spoken, the information must be read as related to that specific group and period and cannot be generalized to represent the voices of all Latino youth. Lastly, an additional delimitation is the already established relationship between the participants and the researcher. The researcher had been the participants' teacher for at least a year and had developed a level of trust and intimacy with them that would be unavailable to an outsider.

Definitions of terms are deemed necessary in order to assure a collective understanding of certain key words used throughout this study. By using the definitions from the literature to which this study is connected, the relationship between this work and a broader field of knowledge is made evident.

Banking education: According to Freire, *banking education* is an approach in which the teacher becomes the depositor of knowledge, which the students as empty vessels passively receive. Such knowledge is memorized and regurgitated: "Instead of communicating, the teacher issues communiqués and makes deposits" (1970, p. 58).

Conscientization: The concept of *conscientization* is central to Freire's epistemology, and implies a process through which individuals transcend the apprehension of reality in order to critically analyze it. As Freire stated:

> Se cree...que soy yo el autor de este...vocablo *concientización* debido a que es el concepto central de mis ideas sobre la educación. En realidad, fue creado por un equipo de profesores hacia los años 64; se puede citar entre ellos al filósofo Álvaro Pinto y al profesor Guerreiro...me dí cuenta...de la profundidad de su significado, porque estoy...convencido de que.... La concientización implica que uno trascienda la esfera espontánea de la aprehensión de la realidad para llegar a una esfera crítica en la cual la realidad se dá como objeto...y en la cual el hombre asume una posición epistemológica...la concientización es

compromiso histórico y...está basada en la relación conciencia-mundo. (1974, pp. 29-30)

> It is generally believed that I am the author of this strange word *conscientization* because it is the central theme of my ideas on education. In reality, it was created by a team of professors, among them the philosopher Alvaro Pinto and Professor Guerreiro around 1964. Upon hearing the word *conscientization*, I immediately realized its significance because I am totally convinced that education for liberation is an act of knowing, a critical approximation to reality.... Conscientization implies that one transcends the spontaneous sphere of the apprehension of reality to arrive at a critical sphere in which reality exists as an object...and in which man [and woman] assume an epistemological position.... Conscientization is a historical compromise and...is based in the relationship existent between conscience and the world. [translation mine]

Dialogue: The term *dialogue* encompasses a desire to mutually interrogate the meaning of reality in order to transform it. As defined by Freire, dialogue is "the encounter between men [and women] mediated by the world, in order to name the world" (1970, p. 76).

Hidden curriculum: Even though the concept of the *hidden curriculum* was coined by Jackson (1968) and is understood as the unspoken words and climate existent within the educational system, Giroux's definition is utilized in this study since it addresses "the norms, values, and beliefs embedded in and transmitted to students through the underlying rules that structure the routines and social relationships in schools and classroom life" (1983, p. 47).

Latino: In this study, the term *Latino* is used because the term *Hispanic* was contrived by the officials of the U.S. government as an encompassing term that places all Latinos in one category and "its connotation provides links between Spanish colonialism and modern day imperialism...[denying] ethnicity, culture, and linguistic variation as well as historical and present day struggles of diverse people" (Walsh, 1991a, p. 84).

Participatory research: This type of research entails the active participation of the community in analyzing its own reality in order to transform it. According to Vio Grossi it is an "educational and action-oriented activity...that could resolve the continual tension between the process of knowledge generation and the use of that knowledge, between the 'academic' and the 'real' worlds, between intellectuals and workers, between science and life" (1981, p. 43).

Praxis: The term *praxis* is grounded in Marx's theoretical work and further illustrated in the work of Gramsci (1971). It encompasses a process of action and reflection that may result in transforming reality (Freire, 1970). Walsh (1991b) defined praxis as a continuous process of action that demands reflection, service, and love.

Praxis-oriented research: This process can be defined as "activities that combat dominance and move toward self-organization and push toward thorough going change in the practices of...social formation" (Benson, 1983, p. 338).

Problem-posing education: Freire argued that problem-posing education is a process through which individuals critically perceive their reality and attempt to transform it. Furthermore, problem posing is "dialogical...constituted and organized by students' view of the world, where their own generative themes are found" (1970, p. 101).

Qualitative activist research: This type of research aims to facilitate "a set of institutional processes that will generate contexts for change, document processes of change, and create the conditions for participants to engage in ongoing reflection on changes" (Fine & Vanderslice, 1992, p. 206).

Socio-drama: The technique called *socio-drama* is defined by Walsh as "a dramatization of a plausible (but fictional) social situation [which enables students] to depict and recount the struggles, conflicts, and meaningful issues of their lives without having to personally reveal themselves" (1994, p. 221).

Voice: According to Walsh, *voice* is "the speaking of consciousness and the speaking to reality...voice cannot be considered an individual phenomenon but must be seen as the product and process of society, identity, and reality" (1991a, p. 37).

CHAPTER TWO
Rupturing the Structured Silence

As stated before, the subordination, suppression, and silencing of bilingual students' voices and their communities by the educational system have come under scrutiny during the past decade (Darder, 1991; Walsh, 1991a). This study seeks to provide a forum for students' voices by examining some of the factors that promote the silencing of voice in Latino high school students and submerse them in the culture of silence (Freire, 1985; Shor & Freire, 1987). It explores how students perceive their cultural and linguistic reality, their family history, and their home experiences within the educational system. It also looks at what students foresee as alternatives for promoting educational reform, aiding the emergence and legitimization of their voices, and attempting to deconstruct practices that tend to encode privilege, power, and marginality in the public school system. Perhaps when the educational system listens to students' voices it will become a democratic sphere, thus opening up the encoded structure of silences often imposed on the less privileged (Weis & Fine, 1993).

The review of the literature is divided into three sections. The first section presents studies that offer insight into the factors promoting the subordination, suppression, and silencing of Latino students' voices and their communities within the educational system. Section two reviews studies that describe students' perceptions of their cultural and linguistic reality and examines what happens when their voices emerge. Section three covers studies discussing alternatives that can promote the emergence and legitimization of voice, thus providing a course of action.

During the past four decades, education in America has been the subject of many studies (Amidon & Flanders, 1963; Jackson, 1968; Kliebard, 1966; Medley & Mitzel, 1963). Reports about the condition of American schools have abounded, and major reform documents have been presented, including *A Nation at Risk: The Imperative for Educational Reform* (National Commission on Excellence in Education.

1983), *A Place Called School: Prospects for the Future* (Goodlad. 1984), *A Nation Prepared: Teachers for the 21st Century* (Carnegie Corporation. 1986), *Tomorrow's Teachers* (Holmes Group. 1986), and *College: The Undergraduate Experience in America* (Boyer, 1987). Such documents depict America's youth as a homogeneous group composed of white, middle-class students who live in the suburbs, thus implying that students of color living in the inner city have no different needs (Passow, 1984). These documents view education as a way of marginalizing and silencing the voices and histories of children of color, whose experiences are discounted as unworthy of notice (Giroux & Simon, 1988).

Poplin (1991a) proposed that there are two competitive bodies of literature attempting to promote educational changes: the excellence/reform/effective schools movement and the transformative movement. The excellence movement reflects research that equates effective teaching practices with increased time on task and higher achievement test scores. It concentrates on "reductionist" pedagogical practices, such as teacher-student interaction, amount of time on task, objectives and outcomes, and the reproduction of a curriculum geared to the academic success of the dominant group. Neglected are issues of privilege and power that aid the development of silence (Weis and Fine, 1993). The transformative movement attempts to define new approaches that adapt newer views of the world (Poplin, 1991a). Poplin distinguished three spaces within this continuum: constructivism, critical pedagogy, and feminine pedagogy, all of which share, in common, a desire to incorporate new and different approaches to education while departing from the "back-to-basics" trend.

Three subareas of literature identify the reasons why traditional back-to-basics approaches may promote the silencing of voice. They refer to this reductionist approach as the selected policies, practices, and discourse that promote and structure the suppression of voice. The three subareas are teacher-student interaction and its impact on student achievement; the role of the hidden curriculum; and the consequent absence of dialogue. A description of each area is necessary to comprehend how deeply they are embedded in the traditional approach to education and how they work to perpetuate the unequal distribution of power and the silencing of voice within the educational system.

Reformists continue to emphasize the lack of teacher-student interaction as one of their most salient concerns. In 1970, Silberman stated that in most classrooms observed, teachers did most of the talking, thus limiting communication between them and their students (p. 73). The analysis of teacher-student interaction has been the subject of a great deal of observational research for over thirty years, but especially during the 1960s (e.g., Kliebard, 1966; Bellack, Kliebard, Hyman, & Smith, 1966; Medley & Mitzel, 1963; Flanders, 1962; Amidon & Flanders, 1963; Hough, 1967; Jackson, 1965; Hughes, 1963; Baker, 1986; Cornbleth & Korth, 1980). Most of the studies concentrate on the amount of time a teacher spends questioning, praising, or correcting students. Unfortunately, many studies have revealed that teachers praise low achievers less often, criticize them more frequently, allow them fewer opportunities to answer questions, and give them less time to respond (Good, 1987).

In 1971 the U.S. Commission on Civil Rights presented its findings based on a study of 400 classrooms including Mexican-American students. This study found that Latino children received more attention than other students in only two types of interaction: giving directions and criticizing. The report also documented the following facts. In the areas of development of ideas, praise, and positive response, teachers engaged Mexican-American students approximately 40% less often than Euro-American students. Similarly, teachers asked questions of Latino students 21% less often than they did of Euro-American students.

Ortiz (1988) reported on a 6-year study carried out in 97 bilingual and monolingual classrooms containing Latino students. The findings suggested negative attitudes toward Latino children among teachers who failed to include these children in activities and avoided interaction and eye contact with them. When Latino students disproved the teachers' expectations of their ability, the teachers often acted in a resentful and suspicious manner. In 1992, the American Association of University Women (AAUW) reported that teachers often treat minority students and Eurocentric students differently. An extensive body of research corroborated this finding.

The academic achievement of students appears to be directly affected by teachers' expectations (Smey-Richman, 1989). A number of studies attest to the fact that teacher expectations of student achievement are often influenced by students' socioeconomic background, race, class, conduct, and ability to perform on tests (e.g., Cecil, 1988; Crowl, 1971; Dusek & Joseph, 1983; Gaines & Dairs, 1990; Kenealy, Neil, & Shaw, 1988; Williams & Muehl, 1978). Expectations for students of color are often lower than for others: teachers see these students as less capable. Darder (1991) provided a clear analysis of the roots of teachers' expectations by delineating the way in which attitudes related to race, socioeconomic background, class, and ideology influence the way teachers perceive students and predetermine their academic performance.

Extensive research on the effect of teachers' expectations on student achievement has been carried out during the past 40 years (e.g., Coladarci, 1986; Campbell & Simpson, 1992; Didham, 1990; Gardner & Mueller, 1984; Good & Brophy, 1969; Hadley, 1954; Hoge & Butcher, 1984; Patriarca & Kragt, 1968; Rist, 1970; Rosenthal & Jacobson, 1968; Rubovitz & Maehr, 1973). Most studies corroborated what Merton (1948) defined as the "spacious validity" of the self-fulfilling prophesy phenomenon, which stressed that individuals respond primarily to the meaning rather than to the objective features that a given situation has for them. Students perform according to teachers' expectations both academically and behaviorally. Teachers' expectations directly affect students' performance (Silberman, 1970).

Rosenthal's Pygmalion experiment (Rosenthal & Jacobson, 1968), perhaps the best known and most replicated study in this area, intended to show that if teachers raise their expectations of students' intellectual ability, the students' achievement will increase. Even though the hypothesis was correct, some defective and contradictory data was provided at the time, and the conclusions were not corroborated by the data (Thorndike, 1969). Rosenthal's continued research was the basis of an updated report, which was presented in 1991. It provided a meta-analysis of 448 studies on the interpersonal expectancy effect in which the findings were corroborated by the data. Rubovitz & Maehr (1973) replicated Rosenthal's study to observe the effects of teachers' expectations on the performance of African-American and Euro-American students. He noted that Eurocentric students were given preferential and more encouraging treatment than African-American students, who were often ignored. Similar findings were reported by Cornbleth and Korth in 1980.

While traditional education understands the concept of the hidden curriculum as a construct of climate, unspoken words, and actions that are part of the transmission model (Jackson, 1968), the transformative theorists see the hidden curriculum as a set of values of the status quo being covertly imposed on students. Giroux defined the hidden curriculum as "those norms, values, and beliefs embedded in and transmitted to students through the underlying rules that structure the routines and social relationships in schools and classroom life" (1983, p. 47). Other authors, including Parsons (1959), Dreeben (1968), Jackson (1968), Vallance (1973/1974), Carnoy and Levin (1976), Apple and King (1977), and Giroux and Penna (1979), have explored the origins, causes, and effects of the hidden curriculum in education. Giroux's study outlined three approaches, the traditional, the liberal, and the radical. Giroux's analysis showed what is lacking in the three approaches: "a view of the hidden curriculum that encompasses all the ideological instances of the schooling process that 'silently' structure and reproduce hegemonic assumptions and practices [and that]...will provide the foundation for using the schools as important sites to wage counter-hegemonic practices" (1983, p. 71).

Palmer (1983) saw the hidden curriculum as perpetrating the passive role of the students. Without being allowed to examine, reflect, and act to transform the socioeconomic forces that shape their destiny, students of color repeat the vicious cycle of violence and poverty that exists in their surroundings, thus perpetrating the self-fulfilling prophesy of academic failure. The role of the hidden curriculum in the education of adolescents appears to be clear. In a covert manner, it seems to dictate norms of conduct, cultural values, and beliefs that exist within the dominant school groups. Often, students are forced to compete against one another instead of being allowed to work cooperatively as a community of learners. Manipulation of students takes place and, with the inner self unexamined, the focus of study is placed on the outside. By excluding minority views, the hidden curriculum constitutes a barrier or a means of isolation, creating an atmosphere of exclusion and marginalization. Transformative theorists have argued that educators and students must be aware of the causes, existence, and effects of the hidden curriculum in order to critically analyze it and make it work toward the total development of young people. Not a simple task, it involves looking at different aspects of education within the school and denouncing practices that serve the interests of only a few.

Understanding the importance of dialogue used in the classroom necessitates a discussion about the differences between dialogue and conversation or verbal interaction. Gitlin provided an analysis of the difference between dialogue and conversation and stated: "Dialogue does not pit one actor against another but rather enables participants to work together to understand the subject being discussed" (1990, p 447–448).

Although this study focuses on *dialogue*, a very specific form of interaction, it bears note that American classrooms lack conversation. The absence of verbal interaction between teachers and students has been carefully scrutinized by Goodlad (1984), Sizer (1984), and Silberman (1970), among others. In an appalling manner, teacher-talk dominates 70% of the instructional time spent in verbal interaction. Most of the talk flows from teacher to students and does not allow student-talk to occur (Sirotnik, 1981). Goodlad (1984) observed that, on average, approximately 75% of class time was spent on instruction. Of that time, 70% flowed as "talk" from teacher to students. He also noted that teachers out-talked the entire class of students by a ratio of three to one.

Basing his comments on an observational study that included over 1,000 schools, Sirotnik (1981) noted that such an approach was in direct response to the increasing pressure to raise scores on standardized tests. Additional findings corroborated previous research done by Goodlad in the 1960s involving 260 classrooms. The results, reported by Silberman (1970), include teaching predominantly by telling and questioning by the teacher, with children responding individually or in chorus. Children learn to assume a passive role within the classroom in order to succeed. By dominating the classroom, most teachers allow students no option except passivity. According to Shor, "teacher talk is one way to deny the diversity of the students, because the differences of the students are bewildering, threatening, or demanding" (1992, p. 103).

In 1984, Sizer reported that within the American classroom there was an almost total absence of dialogue. He stated that, at most, conversation exchange was limited to one or two sentences. Similarly, Ramirez (1991) found in his national bilingual study that in over half of the interactions that teachers have with students, students produce no language since they are only listening. This lack of verbal interaction or conversation within the classroom tends to exacerbate the covert conditions that lead to the absence of dialogue.

Whereas Goodlad, Sizer, and Sirotnik concentrated their studies on verbal interaction, or the outward utterances of speech exchanged between students and teacher, Freire went one step beyond and defined dialogue as "the encounter between men [and women], mediated by the world, in order to name the world" (1970, p. 76). He recognized the importance of mutual understanding and the desire to create new knowledge as equals, as an intrinsic part of the process of liberation of the self, departing from "naming the word" in order to "name the world."

As a result, dialogue takes precedence and becomes a particular profile of the teachers, students, subject matter, and setting (Shor, 1992). Gadamer (1975) implied that mutual respect and understanding must be present in order for dialogue to be meaningful. This is particularly important in the event that one individual possesses more understanding of the situation than the other. The absence of dialogue, or what Poplin called "the paucity of language experienced by students" (1991a, p. 33), in the classroom relates to the excessive use of "frontal teaching" or teacher-controlled talk. Freire hypothesized that absence of dialogue leads to students' immersion into the culture of silence where they are led "to absorb an alien, desiccated, sterile memory fabricated by the oppressor, so that they will resign themselves to a life that isn't theirs as if it were the only one possible" (Galeano, 1973, p. 288).

Shor and Freire (1987) delineated two basic dimensions within the culture of silence: students' internalization of the passive role assigned to them within the traditional classroom, and their aggressive reaction to this role. Walsh (1991a) addressed the causes of silencing as both a covert and an overt reaction on the part of the students, stating that silence could be viewed as a form of resistance or a personal decision not to disclose oneself. Observing this situation, Goodlad (1984) concluded that many teachers opt to maintain a flat emotional tone as a means to control the class, thereby curtailing exuberance, abrasiveness, and praise. Developing an emotional flatness subtracts from the affective domain and adds to the conditions that foster passivity and resistance on the part of students, submerging them in the culture of silence.

In 1891, José Martí expressed similar concerns about the absence of love and the excessive emotional flatness that he observed in American classrooms during his years of exile in the United States (Agramonte, 1991). Almost a hundred years later, Maxine Greene noticed the lack of passion in the classroom. Calling for change, she encouraged teachers to abandon total reliance on the cognitive and move toward affirming intuition and passion through the body (Poplin, 1991b). Moving in that direction would encourage students to become less passive and more willing to engage in dialogue within the school sphere. Horton and Freire have summarized the difficult task that educators face in creating an atmosphere that fosters the joy of learning instead of immersing students in the culture of silence: "the great difficulty...is how to make education something which, in being serious, rigorous, methodical, and having a process, also creates happiness and joy.... I cannot understand a school which makes children sad about going to school" (1990, pp. 168–172).

Freire (1970) named "banking education" as a teaching approach in which the teacher holds all knowledge and the students receive this knowledge. Leading students to memorize mechanically, this type of education becomes an act of depositing. Students receive, file, and store the deposits. Martí denounced this approach when he stated:

> Son las escuelas meros talleres de memorizar, donde languidecen los niños año sobre año...los atiborran en estas escuelas de hileras de números, de datos de ortografía y definiciones de palabras. Y así, con una instrucción meramente verbal, ¿podrá afrontarse la existencia en este pueblo activo,...que es toda de actos ? (quoted in Agramonte, 1991, pp. 57–59)

> Schools are mere memorizing shops where children become languid, year after year.... They fill them up with lines of numbers, spelling rules, and word definitions. And in such a way, with a mere verbal type of instruction, will they be able to face existence in this active world,...which is based on actions? [translation mine]

Walsh (1991b) addressed "banking education" in similar terms. The "banking" system of education perpetuates the myth that knowledge is possessed solely by the teacher, who gives it away to the students. In this manner, the students passively receive knowledge and never discover that they also can teach the instructor (Freire, 1970) In a manner resembling Freire's concept of "banking education," Kliebard referred to the "recitation mode," where the teacher dominates the talk while the students passively absorb this knowledge. By promoting the teacher to question-asker and relegating the students to responders, teacher dominance in the classroom is assured. Students asking questions, addressing one another rather than the teacher, or engaging independently in discovery practices might introduce the risk of an uncontrolled environment and threaten the essence of the school structure (Kliebard, 1989). Kliebard argued against the unidirectional approach in education that stresses having the teacher provide the information without allowing the students an opportunity to interact (Kliebard cited in Faltis, 1990). His theory reinforced what Freire (1970) described as the utilization of the banking concept of education to diminish the creativity of the students, thus promoting domination. Shor (1992) argued that teachers who lecture or use worksheets sometimes do so to gain a protective distance from the students.

A number of authors have addressed students' resistance to banking education. Shor, for example, spoke of how this resistance might be expressed as "passivity, resentment...sabotage, silence, submission, playing dumb, getting by, dropping in and out of courses, not doing homework, coming late, being absent" (1992, p. 216). McLaren suggested resistance might mean "to fight against the monitoring of passion and desire...a rejection of...reformulation as docile objects where spontaneity is replaced by efficiency in compliance with...needs" (1989, p. 188). Giroux defined resistance as "a personal space, in which the logic and source of domination is contested.... [It] functions as a type of negation or affirmation placed before ruling discourses and practices" (1988, p. 162). According to Darder, "bicultural students participate in oppositional behaviors that are centrally linked to the act of resisting the dominant ideological patterns of knowledge and relationships of power which are in direct conflict and contradiction with their lived experiences" (1991, p. 43). As McLaren pointed out, such resistance might be "a form of moral and political indignation...in order to survive with a measure of dignity the vagaries of class and cultural servitude" (1989, p. 202).

Walsh posed crucial questions that must be addressed within an educational setting if the process of educational change is to be analyzed. Among them are: "What does it mean to really make a difference in schools? Who should be the actors and what should be the substance of educational change? What does educational change and making a difference signify and suggest?" (1996, p. 72). As Nieto (1994) pointed out, listening to students' voices is the beginning of a process to reform school policies and practices. Unfortunately, most studies do not include the students' perceptions of the problems, thus creating a gap. The students' point of view is never taken into consideration, the students' voices are not allowed in the discussion, thus making students the invisible, silent, marginalized partners in education. A brief examination of four studies reveals how students' perceptions and voices may be used as a springboard to explore the realities existent within the school system. These studies promote different approaches to and different understandings of the substance of educational change. They also provide an important backdrop for this research study and are summarized below.

Poplin and Weeres (1992) carried out a study as part of the Claremont Graduate School Project that hails as one of the few large-scale studies of its kind. Using a participatory approach, they elicited responses from students, teachers, parents, and the community. Their study is based on the premise that the most important aspects of education happen in the classroom because the primary experts are those who work there. Based on a one-year study of 4 schools in California, the report included 160 meetings, 4 retreats, 24,000 pages of transcripts, 18 hours of videotape, and 80 hours of audiotape. Poplin and Weeres identified a number of classroom issues as a result of their interviews with students of multiple ethnicities.

Their findings highlighted seven issues that participants found to be key: (1) relationships, (2) race, culture, and class, (3) values, (4) teaching and learning, (5) safety, (6) physical environment, and (7) despair, hope, and the process of change. Each issue includes areas of concern that point to the need to listen to students' voices. Each area details the issues considered most important by students.

According to the students, care and a desire for authentic relationships ranked foremost in the area of relationships. Getting to know the students would promote a better understanding and the development of trust, which in turn would foster a desire to perform better.

> Teachers should get to know their students a little better, not to where they bowl together but at least know if they have any brothers or sisters. I have found that if I know my teacher I feel more obliged to do the work so I don't disappoint them. Once my trust is gained I feel I should work for myself and also for the teacher. (quoted in Poplin & Weeres, 1992, p. 21)

Seen as part of the school life by students, racism and sexism constantly occurred in the form of name-calling. Children of color referred to the struggle they faced in negotiating two or more cultures; they need more classes that will help them comprehend their cultures, histories, and past:

> Classes would be more interesting if they would make it fun and relate subjects to things going around us. It would help us understand and want to learn. And I would like to know about my history, MEXICAN HISTORY! I know I live in the U.S. but I still want to learn about my background. The only way I learn of my background now is by my parents. (p. 10)

Children attending middle school talked about heroes and heroines; they raised their parents to that status often. Students listed their parents' hard work and sacrifice as their most heroic qualities. Other family members appeared frequently, reinforcing the important role that the family plays in the development of children's character.

Current academic tools such as curriculum, materials, and texts appeared irrelevant and failed to challenge students. Participants ranked the memorization of items that bore no relation to daily life as a major concern. The students constantly referred to boredom resulting from practices not grounded in their realities. They voiced a desire to actively participate in the development of activities that reflect choice, relevancy, and reflection: "I dislike the unuseful teachings that have nothing to do with [the] everyday life of my future. Things I can just look up in a book I have to memorize" (p. 36).

> My teacher just lectures and gives the assignment and then spends the rest of the class period behind the desk. He has no regard for me as a person but just sees me as another student to be stereotyped. I'm black female, African-American in the eleventh grade. (p. 36)

Participants in this study listed specific concerns in the area of school safety. Many students admitted that they considered their campus to be a violent place: "I dislike having to attend a school where there is so much violence. Our school has a big gang problem. At times I don't feel I'm safe, which is my constitutional right!" (p. 33). Students were afraid of stereotypes and ignorance as the common cause of prejudicial remarks.

Deeply concerned with issues of overcrowding, and the lack of proper restroom facilities, personal space, and aesthetically pleasant surroundings, students commented that these conditions occurred more frequently in schools with little or no air-conditioning and in schools located in low income areas:

> I would make my school with enough rooms so that you don't have 40 or 50 kids in class. I would put comfortable seats in there, a coat rack in each class so your jacket won't touch the floor and get all dusty. And I wouldn't have the bathrooms on the other side of the school. (p. 35)

Students described racism, poverty, unemployment, and community violence as the main sources of despair. Some students experienced a sense of hopelessness in regard to their own situation: "This place hurts my spirit" (p. 11). Another participant stated: "Money should be put in school and not in unuseful things. Our future is being thrown away. The government doesn't really care about the future that waits for us" (p. 37).

Poplin and Weeres confirmed that there are deep and fundamental causes creating the problems identified in their study. They also stressed that "[s]een through multiethnic students' eyes and the eyes of other participants inside schools, the problems of public education in the U.S. look vastly different than those issues debated by experts, policy makers, academicians and the media" (p. 11). Using the participants' voices provided a unique insight into the problems being faced by students and schools today. Outside experts may attempt to remedy a situation, but without considering student voices, their studies will not reflect the reality existent in schools.

Based on results obtained in an action research project, Zanger's study (1994) obtained data through students' discussions, reflections, and writing. Conducted in 1989, this study included 20 Spanish-speaking high school participants living in Boston. They were asked to aid non-Hispanic teachers in obtaining a more complete understanding of the needs of Latino students. Data analysis was conducted through a thematic approach. Three final themes were reported: marginalization, cultural respect, and student-teacher trust breakdown.

Marginalization within the school system was described by the students as a sense of being excluded by peers and teachers who were non-Latino. Students' voices expressed feelings of inferiority and invisibility. Sandra, a Dominican girl, clearly expressed these feelings: "They won't accept you if you're not like them" (Zanger, 1994, p. 176). A boy from Guatemala described the stigmatization experienced by Latino students due to their background, culture, and accent: "They use you as a joke…if you're not wearing Adidas, you're not joined in (p. 176). Like the participants in Poplin and Weeres' study (1992), the students in the Zanger study mentioned issues of care and a desire for authentic relationships. Ana stated: "we like people to think of us as human beings" (p. 179).

Most participants in Zanger's study felt a need to be accepted for themselves. They stressed a desire to have their cultural background and history incorporated into the curriculum as a means to dispel misconceptions based on racism and raise students' status through legitimizing ethnicity. The participants in Poplin and Weeres' study raised a similar concern. Alicia, a Puerto Rican student, said that she wanted to find out more about her own history because "ever since I came here…my ethnic background was like pushed away, and they just want me to be as American as apple pie (p. 180). Elsa, one of Zanger's participants, stressed that teachers could learn a lot from the students, just as students learn a lot from teachers. Elsa used words that also stressed her desire to learn English but not at the expense of forgetting her mother tongue. Zanger described the breakdown of teacher-student trust. Her data provided evidence that some students lost trust in their teachers due to racist attitudes on the part of the teachers, as described by a Puerto Rican boy who stated that the teacher "called me a spic right in the class" (p. 186).

Research shows that there are teachers who think that Latino students are not capable of performing as well as other students. Zanger described this as a bias that educators show toward students who are different from them. Internalizing such feelings, students tend to perform according to teachers' expectations. Alicia stated that some teachers seem to say "oh, they're Hispanics, they can't do as much as the other kids can do" (p. 186). Other students compared the lack of care, support, or true family-like concern on the part of teachers with the teacher-student relationships they experienced in their countries of origin. Citing this weak teacher-student relationship as the reason for erosion of student-teacher trust, Elsa, a Dominican, said, "in our countries, teachers are…friends, families to the students" (p. 187).

Like the participants in Poplin and Weeres' study (1992), Elsa expressed dissatisfaction with the methodological approach used by some teachers. She stated: "Here, the teachers are just 'open the book, read from page 20 to page 30, answer the questions on page 35" (Zanger, 1994, p. 188). Although Zanger conducted her study on the East Coast of the United States, and Poplin and Weeres' research was carried out in Southern California, the data presented through the students' voices showed similar concerns. Zanger summarized her findings by stating that the data portrayed "the experiences of the Hispanic students: their marginalized position in school, the lack of cultural respect shown by the school environment, and the breakdown in mutual trust with many teachers" (p. 190).

Nieto's study (1994), based on the results of interviews with 10 junior and senior high school students, showed academic success to be a common element, despite the fact that students differed in terms of racial, ethnic, socioeconomic, and linguistic background. Nieto stated that all her participants were interested in completing high school and attending college, had good grades, were positive but critical about their school experiences, considered themselves successful, and had made some plans for the future. Four major areas of concern emerged from the students' perceptions: curriculum, pedagogy, tracking and grades, and racism, bias, and discrimination.

Citing the irrelevance of curriculum materials, the lack of cultural representation, and the exclusion of home-based languages and experiences, Marisol, a 16-year-old girl from Puerto Rico, spoke for many of the participants. She stated that she had a problem with one of her teachers who insisted that she should not speak Spanish in class: "I could never stay quiet and talk only English, 'cause sometimes...words slip in Spanish. You know, I think they should understand that" (Nieto, 1994, p. 400).

Thirteen-year-old Fern, a Native American and a junior high school student, expressed concern over the erroneous concepts about her people as presented in her class: "We were reading about Native Americans and scalping. Well, the French are really the ones that made them do it so they could get money. And my teacher would not believe me. I finally just shut up because he just would not believe me" (p. 402).

Similar to the participants in Poplin and Weeres' study, some of the students in Nieto's study expressed a sense of dissatisfaction with the methodological approaches used in school. According to Nieto's participants, most teachers used the transmission model, with routine and rote memorization prevailing over critical thinking. It is important to note that students cared about the way teachers approached their jobs and recognized the difference between a creative and a traditional educator. As Rich stated, "A teacher can make a class interesting. Not like a normal teacher that gets up, gives you a lecture, or...just pass out the work, you do the work, pass it in, get a grade" (p. 405). Another student stressed the need for teachers to be creative. Linda, a senior in high school, expressed the importance of being allowed to ask questions. She also stressed the need for creativity in the teaching field: "there were several classes where I lost complete interest. But those were all because the teachers just [said], 'Open the books to this page'" (p. 405).

The participants made no direct mention of how grouping students by ability or tracking influenced performance in a negative fashion, but they stated that "teachers' expectations often doomed their peers to failure" (Nieto, 1994, p. 410). As previously pointed out, such expectations were usually based on the students' class, culture, and race, and they had an effect on students' achievement. High grades were seen as a means to get more teacher attention and parental gratification. Rich expressed a concern about having to memorize the material without understanding it: "You can memorize the words, you know, on a test...but...if you memorize them, it's not going to do you any good. You have to learn them" (p. 411).

Nieto's participants expressed the same concerns regarding racism and discrimination as Poplin and Weeres' and Zanger's participants. Manuel, a Cape Verdian student, explained the difficulties he experienced in getting along with American students: "It's kinda hard [to] get along with them when you have a different culture, a different way of dressing and stuff like that. So kids really look at you and laugh, you know, at the beginning" (p. 414). Manuel expressed his desire for teachers to become acquainted with their students' background and family history in order to promote better understanding and support. His desire stemmed from his parents' recent immigration to the United States and their unfamiliarity with the educational system. He also spoke about the need for teachers to get to know their students in order to influence them: "If you don't know a student [and] his background, there's no way you are going to get in touch with him. There's no way you're going to influence him if you don't know where he's been" (p. 418).

Nieto's study, mirroring Zanger's and Poplin and Weeres' results, reinforced the fact that students' voices provide a different insight on problems existent in schools today. Such results also addressed the need to include students' views and incorporate them as part of the reform movement. In order to transform pedagogical practices in a critical manner, there is a need "to undertake a total transformation not only of our schools, but also of our hearts and minds" (Nieto, 1994, p. 424).

Walsh (1996) addressed the realities that high school students of Haitian, Latino, and indigenous South American backgrounds face in the American classroom. In contrast to the participants in the studies discussed above, many of the students that Walsh quoted are actually engaged in activist research and work in their own schools and communities. Walsh initiated some of this research and work; in other cases she has been collaboratively involved. The importance of this study rests on the students' perspectives that converge on similar themes: school environment, identity, language, and teaching and curriculum. The students' voices concurred on these issues even though they attended schools in different settings from the East Coast to the West Coast.

Issues concerning environmental safety in schools surfaced in Walsh's study (1996), as they did in Poplin and Weeres' report (1992). Students were concerned about the difference between the real world and what they experienced in school, as well as their personal safety within the school: "We don't feel safe" (Michele, Puerto Rican student, Walsh, 1996, p. 9). Similar comments were made by another participant, Sandra, a 15-year-old Puerto Rican/Dominican student who felt that the school did not take into consideration the real world because they acted as if "the students, the teachers live in a glass bowl or bubble."

Sandra spoke about negotiating identities between groups while taking into consideration ethnic and racial backgrounds: "My identity is me…it's my Dominican side and my Puerto Rican side" (p. 54). The overt and covert efforts to disregard students' identities in the classroom were also explored by Sandra, who addressed the need for teachers to understand the complexities confronted by students who come from bilingual and bicultural families and experience teacher pressure and peer pressure to become somebody else (Walsh, 1996).

Rosalba, a Mexican-American student, addressed the need for schools to acknowledge and include the identities of the students, as well as their home-based experiences: "To be able to function in school you have to dehumanize, be an object." Adalberto, a Dominican student, conveyed similar thoughts by stating that the teachers "need to understand that our lives are much more than just what they see and control in school" (Walsh, 1996, p. 34). Marcela, a Chicana student, explored the possibility that the identities of students were purposely obliterated as part of the system's need to dominate and control: "So in school, our identities are intentionally played down, left out" (Walsh, 1996, p. 56).

Several participants discussed issues of language including how being bilingual separates them from other students, and how, within the bilingual school program, efforts were made to thwart the development of a bilingual linguistic identity. Roberto, an indigenous Ecuadorian student whose first language is Quichua, said, "Sometimes people think the language you speak is who you are" (Walsh, 1996, p. 50), which in his case was not true since Spanish was his second language, not his first. Sandra's words underlined the need for the acceptance of code switching as part of a student's manifestation of identity: "Teachers still think code switching means you can't speak either language" (Walsh, 1996, p. 74).

Like the participants in Nieto's, Zanger's, and Poplin and Weeres' studies, the participants in Walsh's study pinpointed the lack of representation of their cultures and background in the curriculum and textbooks. As José stated: "I don't see myself in none of them books no matter they be Spanish" (Walsh, 1996, p. 86). Roberto's remarks echoed the same feelings: "My indigenous people, it's like we don't exist, everything is from the white, the U.S. perspective" (Walsh, 1996, p. 78).

Adriana's comments pointed to the underlying reasons that perpetuate the unjust social conditions existent in today's educational school system and the ways they can be remedied: "We need to deconstruct the Eurocentric model of curriculum" (Walsh, 1996, p. 70). Walsh's study went a step further, and, through the voices of the students, it examined (a) the real causes that determine how and where bilingual students are positioned within the educational system, (b) the production and reproduction of power in schools, and (c) the different manner in which the educational system works to delimit the potentiality of students of color. It explored the demands, tensions, concerns, and challenges that constantly marginalize and dehumanize students of color who find themselves living in an unjust and non-accessible school and society. It challenged the reader to realize, as Walsh made clear, that the experiences, voices, and struggles of students provide lessons for educators to learn, and that educational reform must consider the real lives of people if it aims to build a society that is more just and democratic in nature. Such reform can mold, shape, and transform students and society by triggering active commitment and social involvement (Walsh, 1996).

An alternative perspective of teaching can be found in Freire's concept of "liberatory education" or the "problem-posing" approach (1970), which perceives society and human beings as "unfinished products in history" (Shor, 1992 p. 35). This approach presents education as a process that encompasses the transformation of students into teachers and teachers into students, which Freire referred to as the reconciliation of both poles of the contradiction (Freire, 1985, p. 59). Whereas the "banking" system does not allow the creation of knowledge as an inquiry process, liberatory education believes that the creation of knowledge comes about through a process of inquiry in which people explore their identity and insert themselves in the historical process of existence as human beings while attempting to transform reality (Freire, 1970, p. 58). In this way, a direct connection between literacy and language is established and learning is grounded in the historical and cultural context of the individuals who attempt to construct meaning based on their personal and social realities (Walsh, 1991b). Learning becomes a process in which teachers and students explore, question, and challenge the existing relationships between power and knowledge (Shor, 1992).

According to Freire, the banking system of education implies that men and women are separate from the world in which they live. Such a dichotomy transforms them into spectators rather than re-creators of their own reality (1970, p. 62). At the opposite pole stands the theory of liberatory education, which states that learning can only occur through direct communication between individuals because "[a]uthentic thinking, thinking that is concerned about reality, does not take place in ivory tower isolation" (pp. 63–64). Liberation in Freire's terms "is a praxis: the action and reflection of men [and women] upon their world to transform it" (Freire, 1970, p. 66). Freire defined dialogue as "the encounter between men [and women], mediated by the world, to name the world" (p. 76). Problem-posing education then allows individuals to reflect together upon the world in which they exist without separating action from reflection and reflection from action (p. 71).

Engaging in dialogue, the teacher-student and the student-teachers may begin to pose problems, reflect upon them, and act in seeking solutions. Teachers and students may empower each other by abandoning the concept of banking education and the more liberal interactive theories and replacing them with liberatory/problem-posing education. Empowerment through critical reflection can then take place (Faltis, 1990). A problem-posing approach to education entails the development of a safe haven where students and teachers may come together and reflect upon their lived realities to create new knowledge, which is one of the goals in problem-posing education. Auerbach and Wallerstein summarized it as follows:

> The goal of problem-posing dialogue is critical thinking and action, which starts from perceiving the social, historical, or cultural causes of problems in one's life.... The first step in promoting action outside the classroom is to transform education inside the classroom. Our role as teachers is to create a safe environment in which students can express opinions and, most important, generate their own language materials for learning and peer-teaching. (1987, p. vii)

In problem-posing education, dialogue is seen as an essential part of the process because it makes individuals engage in the act of reflective transformation (Freire, 1970, p. 71). It allows individuals to critically perceive the way they exist in the world (Faltis, 1990). Centered on the individual's experiences through the process of dialectic retrospection, learning becomes meaningful. It gives students and teachers hope of transforming the oppressive and dehumanizing conditions that surround them in order to create a more just reality.

Although Freire's concept of "problem-posing" education (1970) is seen in the United States as related to the theories of experiential thinkers such as Dewey (1938), Kolb (1984), Jarvis (1987), Mezirow (1981), and Rogers (1959), there is a significant difference in approach. Experientialists tend to view students as being aware of their condition as learners in order to control their own learning. Freire went beyond this point and advocated students' personal liberation through a process of conscientization. Dewey (1938) rebelled against what he considered imposing subject matter on learners who do not have the experience to understand it, a point that is further illustrated by Wilson-Burkett:

> For Dewey...education has to be embedded in the real life experience of the learner.... [It] has to connect with the past of the individual as well as propel him or her into the future.... Experience is the product of the interaction of the individual with his or her environment. (1989, p. 2)

Kolb (1984) also saw learning in terms of the individual's interaction with her or his experiences. He implied that a dialectical relationship must exist in order for the learner to grasp and transform the learning situation. The educator's role results in guiding "the learners in integrating new ideas with old ones. Thus the educator is a manager of the learning process and environment" (Wilson-Burkett, 1989, p. 4). In contrast, Freire (1970) pointed to the need to reconcile both poles of the contradiction between teachers as students and students as teachers. Both educators and learners equally share in the process of creating new knowledge through dialogue. According to Jarvis, "the person does not exist in isolation but only as person-in-society. Hence it might well be argued that the highest end product of learning is the enhancement of the person-in-society" (1987, p. 194). In comparison, Freire considered liberation as one of the most important results of education.

Mezirow's theory of "emancipatory learning" (1981), embedded in the examination of the way in which individuals see reality through critical reflectivity, advocated critical awareness. His concept of "perspective transformation" placed an emphasis on "helping the learner identify real problems involving reified power relationships rooted in institutionalized ideologies which one has internalized in one's psychological history" (p. 18). Freire (1970) not only advocated the identification of the problem, but the analysis of the causes of such a problem. The exploration of alternative solutions to it and the immediate action that can be taken to remedy the situation are also central to Freire's epistemology.

According to Wilson-Burkett, Rogers' theories centered on the contention that "learning is more than the accretion of knowledge, that knowledge needs to be functional, not just retained" (1989, p. 10). Rogers' view of the educator lies in the belief that "the task of the teacher is to create a facilitating classroom climate in which significant learning can take place" (1959, p. 236). The teacher is seen as a resource, not a source of educational imposition. "For significant learning to occur the instructor-learner relationship must be one built on trust and empathy and characterized by an attitude of freedom to learn" (Wilson-Burkett, 1989, p. 11). Similarly, a characteristic that continues to make Freire's work (1970) so poignant is his willingness to talk of love, trust, and hope at the core of the learning process. His recognition of the nature of humanness—as an ability to know and transform in order to create a more equal and just society—remains a source of inspiration for educators throughout the world.

Bringing out the voices of the disenfranchised and disempowered members of the community of learners has been a main concern for critical educators in the past two decades. This movement attempts to draw out the voices of the students to discuss issues that are paramount to the society in general and the community in particular. Educators such as Darder (1991), Freire and Faundez (1989), Freire and Macedo (1987), Giroux (1988), McLaren (1989), Park (1993), Shor (1992), and Walsh (1991b) have made major contributions in this field. Most of their work emanates from Freire's concept of liberatory education and focuses on literacy as an empowering tool for social transformation. A common link is established by a desire to create a more just society where all children are given the opportunity to benefit equally from the educational system:

> At stake here is the willingness of educators at all levels of schooling to struggle collectively as transformative intellectuals, that is, as educators who have a social vision and commitment to make public schools democratic public spheres, where all children, regardless of race, class, gender, and age can learn what it means to be able to participate fully in a society that affirms and sustains the principles of equality, freedom, and social justice. (Giroux, 1989, p. 215)

Various alternative approaches have been proposed to promote the emergence and legitimization of the voices of children of color—and their communities—within the school sphere, by Ada (1992, 1990a, 1990b, 1988a, 1988b), Walsh (1996, 1994, 1993, 1991a, 1991b), Shor (1992), and Darder (1992, 1991). An understanding of these approaches is crucial in order to comprehend how schools dictate who is allowed to speak and what can be said in the educational forum. It also can explicate how educators may work toward the destruction of super-imposed structures of power. A review of such alternatives follows.

Poplin (1993) referred to Ada's approach of "Parents and Children as Authors and Protagonists" as an example of a whole language project that was also liberatory in nature because it provided an opportunity for bilingual children to write about their families, thus stimulating the development of literacy by including the children's lives, communities, home-based experiences and language, and inner-voices. Using the creative method, Ada successfully conducted the Pajaro Valley Literacy Project (1988b) with a group of parents who met to discuss preselected books, engaged in critical reflection based on the texts, and later became "authors and protagonists" by authoring books with their children. This seminal work provided the basis for Ada's concept of parents and children as authors and protagonists. By coauthoring books, the children and their families became directly involved in developing the curriculum, thus breaking away from the traditional structure of power existing in the classroom. As a result, they became protagonists (Freire, 1970) of their own lives and authors of their own reality.

Delgado-Gaitan, in the Carpinteria Family Literacy Project (1992), carried out a replication of Ada's Pajaro Valley study with some variations. The program itself has been replicated with variations throughout the state of California and in various other states. McCaleb (1994) and Andriola-Balderas (1995) conducted studies in areas of California. Similarly, in Florida, Diaz-Greenberg (1995) explored the home-school interaction process and challenged the unequal distribution of power in the classroom. This process involved having the parents and children reflect upon and write their own family histories in book form.

Rooted in Freire's theory, Ada's Creative Reading/Transformative Writing Approach (1988a, 1988b) proposed an active encounter with the text as a critical inquiry process. It entailed a creative, active dialogue between the child and the text (1988a). This approach distinguished four phases: descriptive, personal interpretive, critical analysis, and creative action, which can take place all at the same time or in various orders. The descriptive phase focuses on the basic information presented by the text:

who, what, when, where, and how. In this phase, reading is "a passive, receptive, and in a sense, domesticating process" (1988a, p. 104). Cultural and critical literacy are not taken into consideration and reading/writing remains a functional act.

Adding to Freire the affective elements recognized in feminist theory, in the personal interpretive Phase, "the information received is analyzed in the light of one's own experiences and emotions" (Ada, 1988a, p. 104). Characterized by questions that focus on feelings and experiences, it provides an opening for sharing personal feelings, experiences, and emotions. According to Ada, such a process augments the children's self-esteem because it shows that their home language and experiences are important to the teacher and the members of the class, thereby promoting a better understanding and appreciation of the self (p. 104). Through the incorporation of the affective component, the children's voices and the voices of their families and communities begin to emerge in the classroom. "Cultural validation is not something that is superimposed or added on but forms part of the very core of the process" (p. 104).

The third phase focuses on critical analysis. Once the children are able to compare and contrast, they proceed to analyze problems or issues that evolve from the text: "The questions asked at this level will help the children draw inferences about the information presented: Is what happened valid? Always? When? Does it benefit everyone alike? Are there any alternatives to this situation?" (Ada, 1988a, p. 105). The ability to examine the consequences of the situation presented in the light of self-definition, as well as from a multicultural perspective and concern for social justice, characterizes this phase. Through encouraging children to explore the circumstances that determine their lives, the mold created by society through external definitions is broken, and alternatives may be proposed. In a reflective mode, the critical phase presents a problem-posing approach to the information given and opens up the possibilities of a pedagogy of hope.

The creative action phase aims to promote the discovery of alternatives of change that can improve a situation. It also leads to action, or the concrete transformation of the individual, first, and the student's own social sphere later. In this phase the students are encouraged to "discover aspects of their lives that they can improve...by beginning to assume responsibility for their own lives and for their relations with others" (Ada, 1988a, p. 105). Ada's approach aims to begin what Freire calls dialogue (1970). It promotes the liberation of the self from preconceived definitions and packaged ideas by exploring alternatives and situating the self within the realities of daily life. It aims to make individuals feel that they are free "from the feeling of being trapped by unmalleable, self-defeating circumstances [and to encourage] them to reflect critically about themselves, their world, and the place of education in it" (Ada, 1988a, p. 109).

Walsh's various publications share theoretical and practical approaches that aid the emergence of voice in students. One of these approaches saw "literacy as praxis" and indicated that social transformation and empowerment are the final objectives of literacy (Walsh, 1991b, p. 15). According to Giroux (1991), Walsh's thesis centers on the premise that Latino students' voices are silenced due to the racist language of schooling. Walsh demonstrates "that voice, difference, and culture need to be refashioned through pedagogical practices that both affirm and transform their articulation with categories central to public life: citizenship, justice, and democracy [and] that redefine the interplay of cultures, power, and schooling" (Giroux, quoted in Walsh, 1991a, p. xxvi) by approaching literacy as praxis.

Within this continuum five aspects are outlined by Walsh (p 17–18): education is not neutral, nor is any approach to literacy; a critical approach to literacy must recognize that there are contradictory and complex dynamics involved in the relationships between the school, the community, teachers, and society. When approaching literacy from a critical perspective, the possibility exists for social forms of knowledge, which challenge the ways in which social reality is perceived. A critical approach should help students interrogate and challenge the existent forms of power within the schools. The final outcome should be a deeper awareness and enlightened action.

According to Walsh (1994), her pedagogical approaches aim to encourage Latino students to discuss and write about their lives within and outside the schools, and about ways in which their education could be more relevant to their own lives. Her approaches played a significant role in the development of (bi)literacy and the production of new knowledge. While enhancing self-esteem and engaging students socially and academically, Walsh also promoted critical exchanges, which could result in connecting lived experiences with educational learning. Walsh believed that "it is only those who must struggle with and against domination and for voice who truly comprehend this reality; they are the 'experts,' the insiders who know what oppression is and feels like" (1991a, p. 96). Her approach calls on teachers to look upon students as experts who can enhance the learning process by providing their own insights and incorporating their lived realities. This approach goes against the dominant approach, which sees an expert as an individual who distributes policies and power. Thus, knowledge is dichotomized and valued as a means of control (Walsh, 1991a, p. 97).

In two studies, Walsh utilized the technique called socio-drama, which is a dramatization of a fictional but plausible situation to help students represent their lives without having to provide their names (1994, p. 221), to encourage discussion and reflection of students' realities within and outside the school (1991a). In this manner, students freely made the connection between what goes on in their daily lives and their school writing tasks. This approach allows them to explore in a critical manner their positions in society and the conflicts existing within such a context. Walsh used different visual media in her socio-drama. In one study, Walsh described her classroom experience with the photo novel, "a comic-book like format with photographs rather than caricatures" (1994, p. 222), stating that such a project challenges the traditional curriculum and pedagogy while it also shows the potential that critical pedagogy can provide by placing marginalized students as knowers whose lived experiences are valued as an integral part of the curriculum.

According to Walsh, three major aspects emerged from this experience: (1) theme dynamics and the status of literacy and language, (2) tensions resulting from lived experience and how power is increased through collaboration, and (3) becoming authors and assuming the responsibility involved in authorship (1994, pp. 232–234). One of Walsh's major contributions rests in the third aspect presented above: assuming the responsibility involved in authorship. In this case, students not only become authors but take another role when they become responsible for authorship. At this point an examination of and reflection on the causes that create conflicting relationships between schooling and lived experiences takes place. Collective action may be implemented. Experiencing Freire's concept of praxis (1970)—reflection leading to action—the students may become effective agents of change.

According to Shor, empowering education is "a critical-democratic pedagogy for self and social change…a student-centered program for multicultural democracy in school and society" (1992, p. 15).

Empowering education sees the students' growth as a social, cooperative, and active process in which society and self help discover and re-create each other (p. 15). Within this continuum, the goals are to establish a relationship between personal growth and daily life through the development of critical skills that can challenge issues of power, inequality, and justice (p. 15). Shor described his concern with the effects of the teacher's authoritative voice within the classroom by saying that the teacher's voice often becomes an undemocratic tool that silences the students and prevents critical thought from taking place. According to Shor (1992, p. 95), there are several types of teacher-talk that can promote silencing in the classroom. These include using technical or academic jargon, speaking fast and for long periods of time, talking over the students, asking questions that do not require any thinking, not providing enough time for students to answer, discouraging dialogue, restricting discussions based on the students' experiences, correcting students' speech to make it conform to standard usage, and making little or no effort to include people of color as part of the discourse.

Shor presented the creation of a counter-agendum that promotes a dialogic discourse and breaks away from habits that silence students' voices. As a practical alternative to the anti-dialogic approaches listed above, Shor provided the following suggestions to create a dialogic style of teaching: use no academic jargon, listen to students patiently, encourage students to dialogue about their lives and personal experiences, find out what themes are of interest to the students and incorporate them in the curriculum, allow students to use nonstandard forms of speech, and encourage them to reflect on and summarize their own learning (1992, pp. 95–96).

Based on his classroom experience, Shor proposed several techniques to promote the emergence of voice. His four-phase dialogic practice included the following: (1) pose the problem, (2) reflect on the problem, (3) practice literacy development skills, and (4) elicit class dialogue/group reports (1992, p. 252). By engaging in this type of critical dialogue, students and teachers can challenge the traditional approaches and attempt to create new knowledge based on mutual respect and understanding.

According to Darder (1991), language domination is a crucial factor in the silencing of voice and the prevention of students' participation in school activities. Furthermore, Darder states that the bicultural experiences of students of color are not only negated but also ignored as they are immersed in the dominant culture, thus reproducing the unequal distribution of power already existing in a society where the values of the dominant minority are used as the educational standard for all students, and where the school system annihilates the identities of children of color. Darder based her approach on the belief that a critical theory of cultural democracy should lead to the awakening of a bilingual, bicultural voice and should encourage students of color to become effective agents of change in their schools and communities (1991, p. 48). The awakening of this bicultural voice liberates students so that they may begin to scrutinize and challenge the oppressive forces that deny their voices and to deconstruct the conditioned definitions of their own identity.

When students' bicultural voices emerge, students are empowered to actively participate in the collective voice and the critical examination of their lived experiences (Darder, 1991, p. 70). Through an examination of the experiences of the community as a whole, critical reflection may take place and collective action may be taken to remedy the unequal conditions existing inside and outside the school setting. Students are then enabled to critically examine the oppressive as well as the emancipatory tenets that guide the curriculum and their own experiences (Darder, 1991, p. 96).

Darder called for the transformation of education through the use of an approach built on cultural democracy (1991, p. 97). She proposed a pedagogy that encourages a dialectical view of the world, acknowledges the existence of cultural invasions that exercise a negative influence over students' lives, challenges the political nature of the educational system, and is deeply committed not only to the empowerment but also the liberation of all people.

The creation of such a pedagogy is aided by the examination of issues that directly affect the emergence of voice in the classroom. To assess the practices that already exist, Darder (1995) has offered a series of suggestions that can direct and transform the way in which teaching takes place and are grounded in Freire's epistemology (1970). Darder questions whether or not the curriculum reflects the affective and cognitive learning styles of the students as well as their everyday lives and realities. She advocates giving students the opportunities to engage in dialogue and to include their personal, cultural, and home-based experiences and language. Parental and community involvement in school governance and the critical examination of power relations within and outside the school are seen as essential components in a transformative classroom.

Darder provided a theoretical framework that may be used to reexamine the existent conditions within a classroom. It attempted to correct the present unequal distribution of power. Such questions diametrically oppose the tenets of what Freire calls "banking education," which perpetuates the dominant society's attempt to obliterate the students' primary language, cultural identity, and personal experiences; these are totally marginalized (Darder, 1995, p. 51).

In terms of the initial research questions, the review of the literature clearly points to the existence of certain factors that might lead to the silencing of voice in children of color. Among them are teacher-student interaction, teachers' expectations of students' achievement, the hidden curriculum, the absence of dialogue, the culture of silence, and banking education. All of these factors contribute to silencing students' voices in overt and covert ways.

Research studies that elicit students' voices and incorporate them in their findings reveal that they are an unexpected and often overlooked source of information (Nieto, 1994; Poplin & Weeres, 1992; Zanger, 1994; Walsh, 1996). Students' perspectives speak about issues that are grounded in their daily lives and are relevant to their needs. A common thread that weaves through the reviewed studies is the desire of students to have their voices heard, validated, and honored. Common themes that emerge through these interviews are centered on issues of race, culture, and pedagogical practices.

Critical approaches that provide viable alternatives for the emergence of voice are grounded in critical theory (Giroux, 1983). Such approaches demand a commitment to the struggle for a more equal and just society where all students are given the opportunity to become effective agents of change. Educators committed to such approaches must develop classroom relationships by including the lived experiences of children of color and their communities. They should also create an environment conducive to dialogue and encourage a critical examination of the forces that shape and determine the school curriculum, in the interests of constructing a more just and democratic society (Giroux, 1988, pp. 199–201). Walsh (1992) stresses that such tasks must not be taken lightly since they require time and a sincere desire to become personally involved in the liberation process. Among the responsibilities that Walsh points out are taking risks and remaining committed after the completion of the project, because the relationships created cannot be taken lightly or suddenly ended. Walsh stresses the importance of such relationships by stating that one has to be willing to love, take chances, stay present, and remain committed as a participant in a shared struggle.

Darder (1991) summarized the conditions that characterize the "spirit of hope" needed to undertake such approaches, by stating that one needs to believe in an individual's capacity to become an authentic being capable of transforming the conditions that lead to the dehumanization and oppression of people of color. It is important to stress that no single method or approach was identified as the one formula to elicit students' voices. Each pedagogical approach presented contributes, in one way or another, to the emergence of voice in children of color.

CHAPTER THREE
Eliciting Voices

According to Freire, the use of the banking system in education frequently results in students being rendered powerless. All too often, students' voices are silenced and they are submersed in the culture of silence (Shor & Freire, 1987). As a result, individuals are not given the opportunity to become active participants in their own lives. The purpose of my study is to elicit from Latino students what they consider to be factors that silence their voices in the classroom; to explore how they perceive their linguistic and cultural reality within the school system; and to learn what viable pedagogical alternatives they propose that will aid in the emergence and legitimization of voice. The methodology was designed to actively engage the students themselves in the research process and, in this process, to promote personal and social change. This endeavor required a "Naturalistic" qualitative research approach that would allow the data to flow from the participants' words while, at the same time, encouraging self-reflection and mutual understanding in a natural setting. Mutual trust, reciprocity, and collaboration were preexisting conditions. Entering the community was another condition that had already been met. The researcher had been a teacher at the site for 3 years. Also, she had been the participants' teacher for a period of at least a year. Throughout this time, she had engaged in critical inquiry with her students.

The design of this study is based on the principles of participatory research (de Schutter & Yopo, 1983; Fals-Borda & Rahman, 1991; Gaventa, 1988; Hall, 1993, 1992, 1975; Park, 1993; Vio Grossi, 1981). It also draws from what Lather (1991) calls emancipatory/praxis-oriented research, and Fine and Vanderslice (1992) call qualitative activist research. These approaches share in common the notion of "catalytic validity" (Reason & Rowan, 1981, p. 240; Brown & Tandom, 1987). According to Lather, catalytic validity "represents the degree to which the research process re-orients, focuses, and energizes participants toward knowing reality in order to transform it" (1991, p. 68). Freire described such a process as "conscientization" (1970).

In contrast to more traditional approaches, participatory research aims to tear down the differences between the researched and the researcher by having the researched actively participate in the creation of knowledge and in the development of their own critical consciousness (Gaventa, 1988). It emanates from the belief that education and research are not neutral (Freire, 1973; Westkott, 1977; Reason & Rowan, 1981), and that there is a need for a social science that permits the understanding of the unequal distribution of resources and power, while aiding in the creation of a more equal society (Lather, 1991). By involving the community in analyzing its own reality, participatory research promotes the participants' transformation. This process also aims to promote the reconciliation of the tension between life and science, the world of academia and the real world, and the generation and the use of knowledge (Vio Grossi, 1981).

The following methodological characteristics, according to de Schutter and Yopo (1983, p. 68), exist in participatory research:

- El punto de partida lo constituye la visión de la realidad como una totalidad.
- Los procesos y estructuras son comprendidos en su dimensión histórica.
- Teoría y práctica se integran.
- La relación sujeto-objeto se convierte en una relación sujeto-sujeto a través del diálogo.
- La investigación y la acción (inclusive lo educativo), se convierten en un solo proceso.
- El carácter sincrónico y cuantitativo de la investigación tradicional es reemplazado por una orientación diacrónica y una integración de elementos cualitativos y cuantitativos.
- La comunidad y el investigador producen conjuntamente conocimientos críticos dirigidos a la transformación social.
- Los resultados de la investigación son aplicados de inmediato a la realidad concreta.
- The point of departure is a vision of social reality as a totality.
- Social processes and structure are understood within a historical context.
- Theory and practice are integrated.

- The subject-object relationship is transformed into a subject-subject relationship through dialogue.
- Research and action (including education itself) become a single process.
- The synchronic and quantitative nature of traditional research is replaced by a diachronic orientation and an integration of quantitative and qualitative elements.
- The community and researcher together produce critical knowledge aimed at social transformation.
- The results of research are immediately applied to a concrete situation. (translation in Anderson and Irvine, 1993, p. 90)

Rahman (1991) contended that an immediate goal of participatory research is to give back to the participants the legitimacy and the right to use the knowledge they construct to guide them in their actions. Fals-Borda and Rahman (1991) described participatory research as a combination of political power and liberating knowledge that has, as its final aim, the production and development of a thought process that is sociopolitical in nature, can serve as means of identification for popular bases, and provides the oppressed with leverage that is displayed in struggles, action, and projects. Hall (1992) argued that participatory research leads participants to analysis, creation of alliances, and action by supporting the marginalized voices of the oppressed. Park (1993) stressed that dialogue characterizes participatory research and distinguishes it from other methods of social research because it promotes critical and interpersonal, as well as factual knowledge. Dialogic retrospection, as described and utilized by Kieffer (1981), incorporates some elements of participatory research. It emanates from the concept of phenomenological inquiry and involves "dialogical research" (Colaizzi, 1978) and "reciprocal participation" (Sardello, 1971).

Similar to participatory research, the emancipatory/praxis and activist research approaches, described by Lather (1991) and Fine and Vanderslice (1992), actively involve the participants in a process oriented toward social change. The difference between participatory research, as it has been traditionally understood and described, and the emancipatory/praxis and activist research approach is that, in participatory research, the researcher becomes a part of the community, which is constituted by the oppressed, acts as a catalyst in helping the participants identify and formulate solutions to specific problems, and helps them apply the results of their research immediately to solve concrete situations. A social action component leading to the transformation of the participants' realities and aimed toward the attainment of social justice is incorporated. Lather proposed that emancipatory research encourages self-reflection and the generation of knowledge that is theoretically and empirically grounded. Such an approach encompasses a degree of reciprocity that can be increased through dialogic, interactive, sequential interviews that demand self-disclosure and can lead to the negotiation of meaning (Lather, 1991).

Praxis-oriented research encompasses activities that struggle against dominance, promote self-organization, and lead toward social change (Benson, 1983). Three major interwoven elements are seen as important: reciprocity, validity in its multiple interpretations, and the building of theory instead of the imposition of it (Lather, 1991). A warning is given against researchers with liberatory intentions who tend to impose their theoretical views on the participants in the name of liberation. Also, a clear distinction is made between researchers having emancipatory intentions and researchers obtaining emancipatory results (Lather, 1991).

Qualitative activist research views change as an ongoing transformative process that is self-reflective in nature. This approach encompasses three categories: the transformation of the role of the researcher, the reconceptualization of the collection of data, and the grounding of the theories of social change. The researchers admit the existence of a set of biases that lead, but do not constrain, the process. The active participation of the researcher in the promotion and understanding of the change being studied, in an informative but not narrowing manner, is also expected (Fine & Vanderslice, 1992). Qualitative activist researchers have argued that, by interrupting the monolithic belief in the existence of only one voice, they make the collection of data another strategy to promote change, because it pulls from multiple perspectives and promotes the understanding of diverse views. Involving all participants in the research process shatters the belief in one single ideology, interrupts the belief in positions of right versus wrong, and allows for the flow of multiple consciousness. In such manner, multiple perspectives are discovered and granted the legitimacy that they deserve (Fine & Vanderslice, 1992).

Fine and Vanderslice stated that activist research is committed to the construction of theory at the practice and power level, or what Glaser & Strauss described as "grounded theory" (1967). Qualitative activist research aims to facilitate a process, institutional in nature, that will work toward the generation and documentation of change while, at the same time, creating conditions for ongoing reflection on the change taking place. Such a research process promotes conversations with participants that lead to airing, challenging, and rethinking original assumptions, and it creates a space for new theories and practices to emerge (Fine & Vanderslice, 1992).

My qualitative study is descriptive, dialectic, and developmental in nature. It draws from the theoretical and methodological elements described above, linking educational research and action, holistically. Within the framework of naturalistic inquiry, the nature of reality is seen as a construction of multiple realities that cannot be studied separately and do not lend themselves to the prediction and control of outcomes (Lincoln & Guba, 1985). These multiple realities play an important role in examining phenomena within the framework of their natural setting and must be observed in context and not in isolation. A natural, authentic setting—of which the researcher was a part and which involved the participants in ways that helped uncover multiple constructed realities— was necessary for this study.

Beekman stated that, being within the natural setting, the researcher is able to see the world from the inside, construct meanings and structures jointly with the participants, and discover personal and social realities collectively with the participants. As a result, the interaction with the participants is more effective and personal, offering greater insight into individual perspectives. In such activity, there exists a common horizon (Beekman, 1986), which Gadamer described as a fusion of horizons (Weinsheimer, 1985), and all individuals involved can become connected knowers (Belenky et al., 1986). According to Bogdan and Biklen (1982), treating individuals as if they are research subjects leads them to act as such. In contrast and by involving the participants as active collaborators, this study aimed to engage them in personal, critical reflection to promote understanding of realities and individual growth. The participants confronted, integrated, responded, and aimed to transform their oppressive realities. As a result, a process of change that involved the development of a new awareness (Park, 1993), a more positive self-image, and a capacity to transform (Ada, 1990b) was initiated.

In this study the design was dialectic and reciprocal in nature. This lent itself to self-reflection and mutual understanding while providing a forum for the expression of students' voices. Empowering procedures, such as dialectical, sequential interviews, which would elicit the emergence of voice, were used as part of this research design. As Comstock (1982) stressed, the use of a dialogical approach is essential in research projects that aim to treat participants as active subjects rather than as objects that reify existing social conditions.

Lincoln and Guba explained that the purpose of using interviews is to obtain present constructions of people and events related to their lives, including how they feel about issues, what their concerns are, and what motivates them. The use of interviews allows the participants an opportunity to navigate back and forth, while reconstructing, reinterpreting, and predicting present, past, and future (1985). Bogdan and Biklen stressed that interviews foster the gathering of data that is descriptive in nature and is presented in the participant's own spoken form. They also pointed out that such interviews permit a degree of latitude in pursuing topics and shaping the contents (1982). Patton described depth interviewing as a procedure that probes beneath the surface and provides an understanding of the participants' viewpoint in a holistic manner (1987).

Dialectical sequential interviews constituted the vehicle for communication among the participants and the researcher in this study. The use of dialogue allowed the participants to gather together and actively take part in the process, thus promoting self-inquiry and mutual understanding. Engaging in this process gave the participants an opportunity to explore their realities and express their perspectives. Such an approach was effective in eliciting responses and did not limit the participants to just answering questions or responding to items in a questionnaire; it allowed them to speak in a full voice (Park, 1993). During the design phase of the study, the researcher met informally with the participants in order to validate and refine the proposed research project. The researcher explained to the participants the purpose of the investigation and the way it was going to be carried out. She stressed the need for mutual understanding and trust, and asked that the participants be honest and sincere when deciding to commit themselves to this project. All participants were chosen on a voluntary basis after the researcher described the project to the members of her class.

The researcher developed the research questions independently. After sharing the questions with the participants, she asked them to develop the questions to guide the dialogue. This process was carried out in three steps: (1) Each individual developed a set of questions, which were then presented to a small group; (2) the small group selected the questions that were most representative and shared them with the class as a whole; (3) the entire class discussed the questions submitted by each group and voted for those they wanted to incorporate in each topic.

The set of questions to guide the dialogue were printed and distributed to the participants for final approval. Each participant received a set of questions before the dialogue took place. This was done to provide the participants with an opportunity to view the items and ask any pertinent questions beforehand. The participants were divided into pairs on a voluntary basis and proceeded to engage in the dialogues. A set of general introductory questions was asked so that the participants could provide personal descriptions.

The dialogues took place at "Eastern High School" (E.H.S.), in Traviss, Florida [pseudonyms]. Written permission for the study was given by the principal of the school. In addition, each of the participants was asked to sign a written consent form, as well as to bring a signed parental permission form. Each dialogue was carried out orally, tape-recorded, and then transcribed by the participants. The dialogues lasted for a period of 30 to 50 minutes per session. The time and place were determined by the researcher and the participants in order to facilitate the process. A portable tape recorder was used and each cassette tape was clearly labeled with the name of the participant, time, date, place, and dialogue number. All dialogues were recorded unless the participant requested otherwise.

If, during the dialogue, other topics of concern arose, the researcher and the participants pursued them, since it was of the utmost importance that the dialogue should act as an empowering tool for the individuals involved. Seven topics were covered by each participant, and a total of 140 oral, taped dialogues were carried out by the group. The taped version was transcribed by the participants at home and brought back to class for discussion of the process involved in gathering the data and the changes experienced by the participants during the data gathering process. This discussion was carried out first in pairs, and then by the group. An evaluation of the process, the personal experiences, and the effects produced by such experiences followed. The reflections written as part of the data-gathering process and the personal changes undergone by the participants were given to the researcher. Due to lack of time, the participants did not do specific analysis of the data.

The participants submitted the transcribed dialogues in text form to the researcher. The transcribed dialogues constituted reliable and unchanging information. They reflected events that had happened in the past but that could be assessed and reanalyzed without undergoing any change. Furthermore, they represented an invaluable source of information, which was contextually relevant and grounded in the participants' realities. Also, they were written in a language that was natural and pertinent to the setting in which the study occurred (Lincoln & Guba, 1985). Naturalists approach data analysis in an open-ended, inductive manner rather than in a focused and deductive way. As a result, no hypotheses are posed a priori and the analysis of the data occurs as the inquiry takes place (Lincoln and Guba, 1985). After receiving the text, the researcher applied a thematic analysis. The sequential process detailed below incorporated elements from the approaches used by Kieffer (1981) and Bogdan and Taylor (1975), as well as Spradley's emergent theme analysis (1979).

The first step in the analysis of the data involved reading all the dialogues to gain a general understanding of students' perspectives on different issues. A second reading involved looking for key words that would illuminate different topics of concern. Key terms were highlighted to color code them. The dialogues were separated according to key terms. Each dialogue was reassessed to identify the most significant statements. Reflection and interpretation were necessary to uncover the meaning implied in each identified statement and to determine major themes (Wolcott, 1990). Color coding the statements according to themes (Seidman, 1991) proved helpful to prepare for the next step in the analysis. The major statements of formulated meanings were organized into clusters in terms of themes. The major themes were compared with the original text in order to check for accuracy and comprehension. The revised clusters were then synthesized. The researcher carefully reread the transcribed data and analyzed the themes in terms of the main research questions. She then organized the themes in the same order as the research questions and summarized the results.

The research questions for the study are listed according to the categories presented in the review of the literature. As previously stated, the study aimed to answer the following questions:

1. What are some of the factors that lead to the silencing of voice in Latino high school students within the educational system?
2. What happens when their voices emerge?

3. What do students perceive as their cultural and linguistic reality within the educational system?
4. What are some alternatives that can promote the emergence and legitimization of voice in the educational system?

In order to address these questions, all of the participants engaged in one dialogue per topic over the course of one semester.

The questions listed below were used to guide the dialogue. They were designed to provide support to the research questions, and they served as a forum for the participants to share their daily life experiences and the reality of their lives. The questions gave the participants an opportunity to think and reflect about specific issues and to voice concerns and act upon them.

Participants' Personal Description

1. How can you describe yourself?
2. How does the education that you receive in school help you to know yourself?
3. How does your attendance at school relate to who you are?

The study aimed to answer the research questions by guiding the dialogue in the following manner:

I. What are some of the factors that lead to the silencing of voice in Latino high school students within the educational system?

Voice

What does the word " voice" mean to you?
What does having a voice depend on?
Has anyone ever tried to ignore your voice? If yes, who and when?
How do you feel when your voice is respected/ignored?

II. What happens when Latino students' voices emerge?

Knowledge

What does the word "knowledge" mean to you?
How is knowledge rewarded at this high school?
How do you acquire knowledge at this high school?

Power

What does the word "power" mean to you?
How do you see power expressed at this school?
Who do you think holds power at this school?
How do you think that power can be acquired or expressed?
What do you think is the relationship between power and knowledge?
Do you feel that you have any power at this school? If you do, how do you use and/or express it? If you do not, what are the reasons?

III. What do students perceive as their cultural and linguistic reality within the educational system?

Culture

What does the word "culture" mean to you?
What significance does "culture" have for you in your life?
When did you become aware that you belonged to your culture?
How has your life changed since you found out what culture you belong to?
Have you ever felt proud/ashamed of belonging to your culture? When? Why?
What can we do to prevent rejection or discrimination based on culture?
What can we do to preserve/maintain our culture?

Language

What do you think this school promises as "education" to you?
Do you think that the school lives up to this promise? Why or why not?
Do you think that language is the expression of who you are?
What language(s) do you learn at school?
Do you think that within the languages that you speak there are different kinds of languages? Explain the kinds of languages.
What languages does the school offer to you?

IV. What are some alternatives that can promote the emergence and legitimization of voice in the educational system?

Education

What does the word "education" mean to you? When did you start to value your education?
What is the importance of education in your life and how does it affect it?
Are there some Hispanic students that do not participate in the Spanish for Native Speakers program/do not finish high school? If yes, why?
Is education a lifelong process? Is it necessary? Why?
If given the opportunity to actively participate in the process of designing your own education, what would you do?

Reflection

How would you define the word "reflection"?
Has anyone ever taught you how to think about or reflect on the things you do or you say? If yes, who and how?
Is the process of thinking/reflecting a part of your education at this school?
Are the words "evaluation" and "analysis" similar or different from the word "reflection"? How?
How do you think that you can benefit from reflection?

Eighteen Latino participants, all members of the Spanish for Native Speakers program Advanced Placement (A.P.) language class at E.H.S. in Traviss, Florida, were selected on a voluntary basis. There were 12 girls and 6 boys enrolled in grades 10 through 12. They were categorized according to their first and second language development and literacy acquisition experiences. Weber's two categories (1991) were used to identify the students' language literacy: children who became literate in Spanish at a young age and became literate in English at a later stage, and students whose reading skills were developed in English first. Nine of the participants were bilingual students who came from nations in Latin America and the Caribbean and had only been in the U.S.A. for a couple of years. Nine participants who were born and raised in the United States also participated. Most of them had maintained oral fluency and literacy in the Spanish language through parental contact. The participants ranged in age from 15 to 18 and differed in terms of their national, linguistic, socioeconomic and educational backgrounds. They shared a common desire to complete high school and attend college. Many had known the researcher through Spanish Club activities at the middle school level.

This study was conducted in the Spanish for Native Speakers program (SNS) at Eastern High School (E.H.S.) in Traviss, Florida.

Established in 1981, Eastern High School serves the local community and the adjacent unincorporated areas of Traviss County. Due to county boundaries, students from other nearby areas also attend E.H.S. Designed to accommodate 900 students, E.H.S. had an enrollment of 892 students in its first year (see Table 1). Having experienced tremendous population growth during the past 10 years, E.H.S. mirrors the increase in number of students in the Traviss County schools. Many new housing developments, such as Sonoventure, where many Latinos live, Easton, and Shennon, have been built near the school. As a result of the new housing developments, the school's population began to increase in 1985. In the E.H.S. Annual Report for 1985 the principal reported that the student body had doubled (see Table 2).

Table 1: 1981–1982 Principal's Annual Report on Ethnic Population

Ethnicity	Number
American Indian	1
Asian	2
Black	9
Hispanic	30
White	850
Total	892

Table 2: 1985–1986 Principal's Annual Report on Ethnic Population

Ethnicity	Number
American Indian	3
Asian	20
Black	18
Hispanic	65
White	1556
Total	1662

By 1990 the total school population peaked, and the school serviced 2,052 students. The highest increase in children of color came from the Latino segment, which numbered 217 or almost 10% of the total student body. African Americans, who numbered 55 or 3% of the school population, followed.

In an effort to reduce the number of students attending E.H.S., the school board changed the boundaries by taking away a section of Tipper City. This resulted in a decrease in the number of white students during 1991–1992. The change of boundaries did not affect the Latino and African-American population, since neither group had shown a decrease in numbers as reported in the 1991–1992 Annual Report, included in the following comparison chart (see Table 3).

Table 3: Comparison Chart of Ethnic Population Breakdown at E.H.S.

Ethnic Group	Year		
	1981	1985	1991
American Indian	1	3	2
Asian	2	20	33
Black	9	18	58
Hispanic	30	65	211
White	850	1556	1611
Total	892	1662	1915

Although the Latino population of the school increased from 30 in 1981 to 211 in 1991, the school has been slow to hire Latino staff. A Spanish-speaking clerk, needed to greet and assist Spanish-speaking parents and students, was not hired until 1990. The Latino school personnel included one male teacher, three female teachers including the researcher, one female office clerk, and one female cafeteria worker. One Latina parent volunteer helped in the Media Center. None of the administrators knew how to speak Spanish, and there were no bilingual guidance counselors. This situation continues to exist, despite the fact that the school administrators are aware of the difficulty caused by the language barrier when Latino parents try to communicate with teachers and guidance personnel. Many of the Latino students at Eastern High

School express feelings of frustration due to the fact that teachers, administrators, and guidance personnel do not appear to be aware of the cultural and linguistic barriers that hinder communication between the parents and the school.[1]

The Spanish for Native Speakers program in the county began in 1980. It was designed to provide language arts instruction in Spanish to those bilingual students interested in increasing their reading and writing ability in Spanish or preparing for the Advanced Placement Spanish language exam. The program encompasses four consecutive levels (I to IV/A.P.) to be completed during the four years of high school. Admission to the program depends on a placement test that determines the literacy level of each individual. Completion of at least 2 consecutive years of the program is acceptable toward meeting the state's admission requirement to a four-year college. In 1988 the Spanish for Native Speakers program was adopted at E.H.S. for several reasons: The number of Latino students at the school had increased, and the non-Spanish speakers experienced difficulties when native speakers of the language were in the same Spanish class. Non-native speakers of the language felt intimidated and were upset having individuals who already knew the Spanish language participate in the regular Spanish as a Foreign Language program. During the 1988–1989 year, students who were interested in participating in the Spanish for Native Speakers program were tested, and a level III class was formed with approximately 30 students. In 1989 there were two classes: a combination class for levels I and II, and a combination class for levels III and IV. The program had approximately 60 students.

The program had four separate classes by September 1990, one per level, with a total of 77 students. By the next school year (1991–1992) the number of students enrolled had increased to 100, and there continued to be four classes, one per level. The largest increase occurred in September 1992, when 140 students enrolled. Two sections of level III had to be formed in order to accommodate the number of students involved. During the 1992–1993 school year, there were five classes, one per level except for level III, which had two sections. The number of students grew from 30 in 1988–1989 to 140 in 1992–1993, which represents a growth rate of 400%. The 1993–1994 class count showed

---

[1] The researcher obtained the above-mentioned information by informally interviewing school administrators, teachers, clerks, cafeteria workers, and students at the site.

that there were 181 students in the program, divided into seven classes, with two sections of level II and two sections of level III. Projected enrollment for the years 1994–1995 stood at 210 students.

The school has not kept official records for the Spanish for Native Speakers program. It is considered a part of the foreign languages program. The above information was gathered by interviewing administrators and teachers who formerly taught in the program. Consulting the foreign language department head, who had kept her own personal records of the number of students enrolled by years, helped to consolidate the information.

Portrait of the Participants[2]

1. Yeiza, who described herself as Puerto Rican-American because she was born in New York of Puerto Rican parents, was a 16-year-old junior. She had never attended a bilingual program and barely knew how to read and write in Spanish, but she had been placed in the Spanish for Native Speakers program because of her surname.
2. Alicia, who is Cuban-American, was 16 years old and a junior at the time of the study. She was born and raised in Miami, Florida, but had never attended a bilingual program. Upon entering the program she was barely able to read and write in Spanish.
3. Ryan is also Cuban-American and Miami-born and raised. He was 16 at the time of the study. Ryan had never attended a bilingual program, barely knew how to speak, read, and write in Spanish when he entered the program and, due to his physical appearance, lack of a Spanish name and surname, and excellent English pronunciation, was seldom identified as a Latino.
4. Ana was 15 years old and a sophomore. She was born and raised in Cali, Colombia, and had only been in the United States for 4 years at the time of the study. Upon arrival in the United States she had been placed in an English submersion program. She had attended a private school in her own country, and her love for Latin American literature was evident.
5. Natalia was 17 and a junior at the time of the study. She was born in Argentina but moved to the United States at the age of 2. Natalia had learned Spanish at home, but had never attended a

---

[2] The participants selected the names they wanted to use for this study.

bilingual program. Before entering high school, she had studied one year of Spanish as a Foreign Language in middle school.

6. Anita, a 17-year-old junior from the Dominican Republic, had been in the United States for 5 years at the time of the study. She had never been placed in an English as a Second Language (ESL) program and had never studied Spanish in middle school.

7. Danny was 18 and a senior. He was born in Medellin, Colombia, and had moved to the United States at age 3. He had attended school in the United States since he was 5 and had never been placed in a bilingual program. At age 7 he had been held back in school. Five months later he had been promoted. His mother had taught him how to read and write in Spanish, but he had not studied Spanish as a Foreign Language in middle school.

8. Guillermo was a 16-year-old junior at the time of the study. He was born and raised in Ecuador and had only been in the United States for 4 years. Upon arrival in the United States he had been placed in an English submersion program. His enthusiasm for Latin American literature and culture was always evident.

9. Madeline was 17 and a senior at the time of the study. Born in Florida of Cuban parents, she had been taught how to speak, read, and write in Spanish at home, but had never been placed in a bilingual program. Since she had moved from Central Florida at the end of her freshman year, she was the only participant who had attended a Spanish for Native Speakers program before.

10. Alexia was born and raised in the Dominican Republic, where she attended private school. Sixteen years old and a junior, she had been in the United States for only 4 years at the time of the study. Upon arrival in this country, Alexia had been placed in an English as a Second Language program, where she stayed for four months. Alexia missed her country, so her family let her return to the Dominican Republic for a visit twice a year.

11. Clemencia was a 15-year-old sophomore who was born and raised in Cali, Colombia, and had been in the United States for only 2 years at the time of the study. She had attended a private school in her country, and upon arriving in Florida had spent her first year in an English as a Second Language class. Clemencia was well versed in Latin American literature and culture, and she enjoyed writing poetry in Spanish.

12. Lorraine was a 17-year-old junior. Born and raised in San Juan, Puerto Rico, she had attended a private school and knew some English when she arrived in Florida 5 years before this study. She had been placed in a submersion program upon arrival, but had taken one year of Spanish as a Foreign Language in middle school.
13. Rodrigo, born and raised in El Salvador, was 17 years old and a junior. The newest member in the class, he had moved from San Francisco, California, a year before the study began. Having been in the United States for 2 years only, Rodrigo was still in the English as a Second Language program.
14. Sabrina, a 17-year-old junior from Colombia, had moved from Miami, Florida, two years before the study began. She had never been enrolled in a bilingual program; her parents had taught her how to read and write in Spanish at home.
15. Carolina, a 15-year-old sophomore from Colombia, had been in the United States for only 4 years. She had lived in Miami until Hurricane Andrew destroyed her home. Her family moved, and she began attending the Spanish Speakers program. While in Colombia, Carolina had gone to private school. Her love for reading and her ability to write poetry in Spanish, as well as her acting abilities, were always a source of enjoyment for the group.
16. Damisela was 16 years old and a junior when the study took place. She was born in Colombia but moved to the United States at an early age. Her parents, both teachers in their country, had not taught her how to read and write in Spanish. She had taken one year of Spanish as a Foreign Language before enrolling in the program, and had a great desire to improve her reading and writing skills.
17. Ruben, a Peruvian student who had been in the E.S.L. program since its inception, had spent one year in the Spanish Speakers program when he was a sophomore. A 17-year-old senior, he had asked to return to the program for the A.P. class in order to take the exam and obtain college credits.
18. Pablo, an Argentinean, and a junior at the time of the study, had taken Spanish as a Foreign Language during his last year in middle school. His parents had taught him how to speak, read, and write in Spanish in order to communicate with his grandfather.

The researcher is a 45-year-old bilingual Latina woman who was born and raised in El Salvador and had to learn English as a second language at the age of 17, upon arrival at a college preparatory school in Boston. She had similar experiences in undergoing the process of acculturation in the United States as some of the participants. Her first assignment was the teaching of Native Language Arts in Spanish for high school students in the Bilingual Pilot Program at L. D. Brandeis High School in New York City. Subsequent teaching assignments have taken the researcher to another country, where she taught in a State Department–sponsored school, and to Florida, where she taught Spanish for Native Speakers for the Dade County public schools in Miami. The researcher lived in Traviss County from 1983 to 1994 and worked from August 1990 to June 1994, at the local high school where she taught Spanish for Native Speakers and was heavily involved in organizing Latino youngsters in school and community activities. She also organized and coordinated the Spanish Club and the Spanish Dancers Club, and her students participated in the local and state foreign language competition.

CHAPTER FOUR
Emergent Themes and Emerging Voices

This chapter presents the participants' perspectives, insights, and concerns about the factors that silence Latino students' voices within the school system, the cultural and linguistic realities faced by Latino students in the educational setting, and the alternatives to promote the emergence of voice in the classroom, as determined from a series of in-depth dialogues. A number of authors have spoken of the epistemological need to consider students as subjects who can illuminate the realities of school and of their daily lives. The organizing principle of this study rests on the premise that students are experts whose voices need to be elicited, validated, and heeded. Ongoing dialogue within the classroom encouraged such voices and provided an opportunity to probe deeper layers of understanding and perception. Entering this realm was part of the problem-posing method that the researcher had implemented with most participants for a period of over 2 years. It also included different approaches, previously described in the review of the literature, to aid the emergence of voice.

The dialogic retrospective process culminated in this study. It involved (a) collectively developing a set of questions to guide the dialogues, (b) conducting the dialogues, and (c) reflecting on the experience. Each of the 18 participants chose a partner and engaged in dialogue during one semester. The dialogues were carried out orally in English or Spanish and, if necessary, translated and tape-recorded. Upon transcription of the dialogues, the participants jointly and individually reflected on the contents, sharing their experiences with the researcher and the rest of the group. The researcher collected the transcripts and organized the data by themes. Due to the large number of participants, not everyone's voice is present in each theme.

The participants' comments are clustered around four central issues, which provide an insight into the students' perceptions of their own realities and illuminate areas that students consider must be incorporated as part of the learning process. Furthermore, the participants' perspectives reveal ways in which pedagogy and education need to change in order to provide equal opportunities for all students, regardless of class, race, gender, and ethnicity. The four major themes are (1) voice: rupturing the structured silence, (2) power and knowledge: a direct connection, (3) ethnic identity and its relationship to culture and language, and (4) education as a learning process involving reflection. The themes are organized in the same order as the four basic research questions, thus providing partial answers to them. The four research questions are:

1. What are some of the factors that lead to the silencing of voice in Latino high school students?
2. What happens when their voices emerge?
3. What do students perceive as their cultural and linguistic reality within the educational system?
4. What are some alternatives that can promote the emergence and legitimization of voice in the educational system?

Each research question has been stated directly above the themes that addressed it in order to establish the direct relationship between them.

Voice can be described as an individual's effort to express inner thoughts and feelings. It is deeply rooted in one's past experiences, and it develops as part of a process that involves relating and sharing one's personal and cultural history (Fine, 1987; Shor & Freire, 1987; Giroux, 1988; McLaren, 1989; Walsh, 1991a). Often, students' voices are silenced within the educational setting. Understanding what students perceive as some of the factors that lead to the silencing of voice is the central focus in this section. In order to address this issue, it was imperative that the participants defined voice first, and then explored what they considered were the reasons that led to the suppression of their voices.

Most participants defined voice as the ability "to express one's ideas, feelings, and thoughts, and having them heard and understood" (Yeiza). According to Alicia, having a voice entailed the ability to "speak out about any injustice that may be done to you or any of your peers." Coming to voice was also seen as a political act that could denounce social injustice. Making a difference in society through one's voice was an ever-present concern, as exemplified by Lorraine's comments: "Being able to express your voice means to be able to express how you feel about an issue and make a difference." The power of voice as a political tool to create a better world was directly expressed by many of the participants.

Walsh described an inner consciousness realm of voice, which indicates that one's voice is intimately tied to one's innermost thoughts and experiences (1991a). Such a perspective was illustrated by some of the participants. Ana stated that "voice is an individual's only power to express her inner thoughts and life experiences. Without this tool called voice, the inner self is murdered." Natalia implied that having a voice was a moral right, which should be respected as such:

> To me, "voice" means expressing my views, thoughts and opinions, especially on subjects such as culture, racism, and discrimination. Your voice should be listened to and respected. When this fails to happen, you are being deprived of a moral right.

Ada (1988a) stated that "students are taught to obey, to passively follow rules, without ever questioning...to perform boring, dehumanizing tasks without complaint" (p. 2). A similar concern was expressed by Anita:

> Without voice we would not be able to open up and say what we feel. In other words, we would be like robots, computed to simply do, say, and act as we are told by another person. People cannot live like that, I cannot live like that.

In this case, not having a voice was related by the participants to the denial of individual identity and the desire to have students conform to preconceived notions dictated by those in power. Of the 18 participants 16 indicated that the concept of voice was directly linked to identity. Ryan's comments illustrate this connection:

> Having a voice means to be able to express yourself, to relate your ideas and opinions.... To have that restricted will mean not to have a voice at all. To take away someone's voice is to take away their identity and that's really sad.

Voice, according to the participants, was an essential part of identity and, as such, central to the development of self-esteem.

Students' perceptions of why their voices were silenced in schools revealed an array of variables, ranging from fear to ignorance. Many participants considered most teachers and administrators incapable of understanding and unwilling to understand their needs and concerns. In some cases, denial of reality, as well as negative perceptions, played an important role. Guillermo expressed his feelings as follows:

> They [administrators and teachers] try to silence our voices, in some cases, for fear, fear of us exposing those who try to oppress our race, for fear that we say what we feel.... They are afraid that we will better ourselves. Our voice is very important. Another factor is the ignorance of people who think that we are different, and we can affect their lives. I don't see anything wrong in us trying to express ourselves. We are kind, sensible people who want to help the world with our thoughts, our feelings, our beliefs.... We want to follow our dreams and fulfill them.

Ryan concurred with Guillermo and called for an understanding of the differences between cultures:

> I think they might be afraid of what they don't understand. What's not familiar to them, they, I guess, categorize it as different and improper, so they treat it like garbage. And until they try to understand other foreign or different cultures, I don't think this problem will ever be resolved.

The manner in which students' voices are trivialized by some teachers was expressed by **Yeiza**, who felt that, sometimes, adults did not think what she had to say was important:

> Sometimes they just don't care enough to take the time to listen, they think we are just kids.... I also think that, at other times, when you have an opposing point of view, it can seem threatening to someone else if you speak against them, and they feel out of control when another voice is heard.

Madeline, whose previous teacher had overtly tried to silence her when she spoke about being discriminated against, discussed the denial of reality as a cause for silencing:

> When I am allowed to express my voice, I feel that I am someone. I think that they try to silence us because they don't want to see what reality is really like. They want us to think that there is no discrimination and that nothing is happening.

Similar feelings were expressed by **Alicia**, who felt that there was a need for students to express themselves regardless of the obstacles they met:

> Our voices are silenced because they [teachers and administrators] want to avoid getting the truth. You know, finding out what's really going on behind closed doors. They want to keep it under cover.... When we want to express ourselves we cannot be afraid, we have to go and express ourselves anyway, so that people cannot keep us from saying what is on our minds.

Alexia identified the erroneous perception of Latino students that some teachers and administrators held as one of the reasons for the silencing of voice:

> They perceive Latinos as students that never do anything except misbehave, as students that never get their work done and always disrespect teachers and administrators alike. As a result, they think that we are all like that and that our voices should not be heard because they are not worth it.

Ruben perceived silencing as a way to prevent students from advancing or getting ahead within society:

> It seems to me that it is because people do not like to be told that they are wrong or that they are being unjust with others. They do not want anyone to surpass them in their knowledge, so they try to take away our right to express ourselves by force. Latinos work very hard and try to get ahead, many people here know that, they know that we can do many things that they can't do and that's why they silence us.

The conflicting tension existent within the educational system, which touts the concepts of democracy and freedom of expression as integral parts of American life yet manages to suppress an individual's voice through authoritarian figures was expressed by Anita:

> Whenever I am confronted with a form of authority at school and I have to say what I feel but can't, the agony and hurt I feel makes me burst into tears.... We should all be able to express our voices whenever and wherever we may choose no matter what! That's why we live in a democracy, isn't it?

Authoritarianism was often considered a major deterrent to the emergence of voice. Participants expressed a desire to voice their thoughts, feelings, and concerns within the educational setting. However, teachers were seldom willing to listen for fear of losing control or power. A direct connection can be made between the participants' comments and the findings of studies included in the review of the literature (Nieto, 1994; Poplin & Weeres, 1992; Zanger, 1994; Walsh, 1996), and also the study that describes the teacher as the sole team player in the classroom (Goodlad, 1984).

Central to this section of the study is the discovery of what happens when students' voices emerge within the classroom. A sense of connectedness and an ability to listen to and nurture each other's voices were essential elements constantly observed. Engrained was a deep belief in students' ability to construct meaning from their own experiences and create knowledge. Being able to critically analyze issues of power that related to their daily lives gave the participants an opportunity to express inner feelings. Foremost was the general sense of being in a safe haven where each person's opinion was respected and valued.

A description of how students felt when their voices were elicited and respected served as an introduction. Often the participants' comments equated having their voices respected with feelings of self-worth, importance, and contentment. Having their voices silenced caused negative sentiments, low self-esteem, and feelings of being outcasts. Among the issues uncovered was the relationship between power and knowledge and the way it influenced the suppression of voice.

Having their voices respected in class promoted positive feelings about themselves among the participants: "I feel that I am someone" (Madeline), or "I feel that I am important and I am worth something" (Clemencia). As Ryan stated: "It makes you feel good because you feel more confident about yourself, more confident that you belong, and that you're not an outcast." Alicia's comments reinforced such feelings:

> When my voice is respected I feel, I guess you could say, happy about myself, because I feel confident that I can express my voice when I need to. I'm afraid that if my voice wasn't respected, I wouldn't be able to express myself as well as I would if my voice were respected.

Similar thoughts were expressed by Yeiza: "It makes me feel good, important, and respected that someone takes enough time out to listen to how I feel about something." For Guillermo, having others respect his voice led to "an indescribable feeling, a sense of betterment, as if I have completed something good by expressing what I feel and being able to send my message to other people."

The covert attempts made to suppress students' voices in some classes, as well as the efforts to elicit his voice in the Spanish class, were recounted by Ryan:

> Even though I am Hispanic and my other teachers over the years have locked my voice, in this class, I have a voice. I am allowed to express my ideas and opinions. It's like a whole different world. A world where my voice matters, and my opinions really count, because there is a key, the key to unlock everyone's voice. Even though some people are afraid of this key, my teacher inspires us with her ways of teaching, she encourages us to unlock that voice and share it with the world.

Danny expressed similar concerns and addressed the students' desire to express their own feelings:

> In all my other classes I don't have a voice to express my feelings and experiences. Here in this class I finally have a voice. A voice to speak and think what I feel...to really have an involvement in class issues and discussions.

> Having a voice has made my personality grow and has given me a new perspective to learning positively.

Exploring what happens when students' voices are elicited led to a discussion of different issues. Power and knowledge became the focus of the dialogues. Both concepts were defined, and the direct relationship between them was described. The following section presents the students' perceptions on power and knowledge. It stresses the students' sense of powerlessness and teachers' contributions to the suppression of voice, which is often equated with power. The concept of power is often linked to the ability to exercise control over individuals in a particular situation, thus working toward domination and the maintenance of order in society. It usually rests in the hands of the dominant group, which imposes a set of views and rules upon the dominated majority. Power is often not shared with others, thus creating an unbalanced situation, especially in the school setting. According to Freire (1973), it is of the utmost importance that teachers and students work toward reconciling both poles of this contradiction, thereby sharing power in the classroom.

The acquisition of power through voice was at the core of the participants' concerns. They perceived that teachers and administrators might not want students to obtain power, as expressed by Danny: "It is not convenient for them that other people acquire power through voice." Similar thoughts were expressed by Ana, who stated: "Some people don't care and others are afraid of having students gain power with their voices." An undercurrent fear of what might happen if students were allowed to voice their concerns was constantly present in the participants' comments. According to Natalia,

> The word "power" means the inner strength that allows you to make your own decisions. I think the more knowledgeable you become, the more power you have and, as a result, you have more insight on how to use it productively.

Yeiza summarized the participants' general feelings by stating: "We are silenced because people are fearful of our ideas and the power we might obtain with our voices."

The hierarchical distribution of power and its influence on the lives of the students was described by Alicia, who felt that she had very little power in the school:

> Power means control. To have power is to have control over something or someone. In this school, power is rarely acquired, it is given. It is held like a chain: The teachers have power over their students, the heads of the departments have power over the teachers, the principal has power over all. It

can definitely be expressed in different ways. I don't feel that I have much power in this school. If I have a problem and I bring it up, it feels like I'm talking to the wall.

Lorraine was most concerned by the unequal distribution of power, which she believed was held by the administrators and barely shared with parents and teachers. Such thoughts left her feeling that she could count only on her voice as an expression of power:

In this school, power is badly distributed. Teachers and parents don't have enough power here, but the administration holds power at this school. Power means the ability to control things that happen in your life, but the only power I feel I have at this school is the right to be heard.

According to Ryan, he had no power at the school because his life was totally controlled by the teachers, who determined his position and dictated what he should do at all times:

To me, "power" means to have an influence over something, to control. Like teachers, they have power over students. They basically run most students' lives for seven and a half hours every day by telling them what to say, what to do, how to do it, where to do it, even where to sit. I have no power here. My life, for this time, is run by my teachers.

Being "under" the teachers' power was how some participants felt within the school boundaries, where they saw power as a form of domination that allowed teachers to punish students. Clemencia's words illustrate such feelings: "At our school, power is the capacity to dominate and castigate people with ease. We, the students, are 'under' the power of the teachers and the school." However, her analysis of the situation led her to believe that, in reality, power rested in the school board:

This power is based on rules that are drawn by the school board so, literally, no one has power at this school because everyone has to follow such rules. The principal has power over the teachers, but the school board has power over the principal.

Essentially, most participants felt that, at this particular school, even though teachers could exercise control over the students in terms of curriculum and class rules, they actually had no power in the final decision-making process.

In many instances, knowledge is seen as a static and fixed commodity, which is held by a certain segment of the dominant society and is then distributed to those individuals who can afford it. Teachers are often considered holders of such knowledge and are entrusted with depositing it in the minds of students. In turn, students absorb the material presented without being given an opportunity to question or explore. Thus, individuals reproduce the views of the dominant society, never interrogating who determines what knowledge is and whose concept of knowledge is represented within the curriculum.

For most participants in this study, acquiring knowledge was, as Freire has described it (1973), not a static but an ongoing process. It was not limited to school hours or books, and it was present in all activities throughout the day and throughout life. This understanding was clearly expressed by Alicia: "Knowledge is experience. You gain knowledge by different experiences in life." According to Freire & Macedo, "human beings constantly create and re-create their knowledge, in that they are inconclusive, historical beings engaged in a permanent act of discovery" (1987, p. 119). Such a process is described similarly by Ryan:

> Knowledge, to me, is something you keep gaining throughout your whole life. It is acquiring experience, wisdom, and understanding. You acquire knowledge every day; from the time you get up to the time you go to bed, you are learning new things, and that applies to the school system also. Going to class all day, doing your work, and homework are only a part of the process, but all other activities are also a part of it.

Lorraine's powerful metaphor described knowledge as the key to power. She also referred to the respect demonstrated by teachers toward students who are knowledgeable: "Knowledge means being mature, free of ignorance, and being wise about matters of life. Knowledge is rewarded through respect from teachers. Knowledge is the key to power." This is similar to what De Vos describes as the need "to experience the behavior of adults who earn the respect accorded them for their mentoring or nurturing others" (1993, p. 251).

According to some participants, the school equated knowledge with high grades, which were rewarded with special awards such as placement on the honor roll, membership in honor societies, and inclusion on the principal's list. Such rewards were often conferred upon those students who performed according to what the teachers considered to be accepted norms and standards. Some participants suggested that a small number of students of color were included in most cases, as tokens, to represent the school's diversity. Extrinsic rewards were often used, thus leading the students to focus on the reward rather than the value of the activity or task accomplished.

A number of authors have argued that knowledge and power are intimately related (e.g., Giroux, 1989; McLaren, 1989). In many instances knowledge is equated with power, and more knowledge means more power. Many participants in this study seemed to believe that power and knowledge were directly connected, and the more knowledge individuals had, the more powerful they could become. As Natalia put it,

> I think that with knowledge you have a better understanding of how to exercise your power better. Being knowledgeable also gives you more power because you need to depend on fewer people, and instead other people begin to depend on you.

Rodrigo felt that power could not be exercised without knowledge: "The relationship existent between power and knowledge is very clear. You have to know when to exercise power, and in order to exercise it, you need knowledge." When referring to the situation in school, Alicia did not see a direct connection: "I don't see much of a relationship between power and knowledge in this school, but outside of school, the more knowledge one has, the more powerful one can be" thus she stressed the difference between the outside world and the world of school.

Ethnic identity is directly intertwined with culture and language. Each represents an essential part of an individual's existence. The annihilation of one or the other can cause a traumatic experience leading to the lowering of self-esteem and self-respect within the inner world of a person. A central part of this study focused on analyzing students' perspectives on their cultural and linguistic reality within the school. Such views systematically converged on issues of identity, thus reinforcing the direct connection between them.

The intimate link between ethnic identity and culture was ever present in the students' comments. It permeated their thoughts and actions, making it central to their development as human beings. A sense of sadness at the school's lack of appreciation of their culture was often expressed. Constantly, a strong sense of cultural identity emanated from the participants' words; culture was often spoken about as an integral part of their lives:

> Culture means who you are...what your identity is, who your family is, basically, where you fit in this world. Well, to me culture means your identity. It describes you and your family and where you come from, which is very important, you should never lose sight of that fact.... Culture should always be

considered as a part of your identity. If you don't, or if you let it go, you are lost. Once that's gone, you can't get it back. (Ryan)

Natalia's words reinforced the concept of culture as an essential part of ethnic identity and the role it had played in her life:

> My culture is important to me because it is a huge part of my identity. My entire life I have been taught to be proud of who I am. My culture is a part of me, I have grown up in this culture and it has helped me identify.... It has also taught me about my history and language.

The crucial role that parents and family play in fostering or suppressing culture and identity, as well as the influence of *familialism*, or the "cultural value which includes a strong identification and attachment of individuals with their nuclear and extended families" (Marin, 1993, p. 184), was clearly identified throughout the participants' words, as Alicia explained:

> Since my family emphasizes the importance of culture, it affects me in many ways. I've known I belong to my culture for a long time, ever since I was a baby, because my first language was Spanish, and so I was brought up with Spanish food, Spanish music. I often spent time with my grandparents, and they were very Cuban people.
>
> Just recently I had a family reunion. It was the one-hundredth anniversary of my great-great-grandparents wedding. There was a lot of food, a lot of music, and a lot of family and people I'd never seen before in my life. They were all from Cuba, you know, and it was all a very interesting experience, and it was about then that it all tied in together, that I belong to my culture, and that I'm happy to be Cuban. That's when I really and truly realized what my culture was about, and it was at the reunion.

Children's enculturation, or "the cultural teaching that parents [and] families...provide to children" (Bernal & Knight, 1993, p. 3) seemed to be carried out mainly by the participants' parents and family, who considered their relatives important agents in this process (Knight, Bernal, Cota, Garza & Ocampo, 1993). As Anita pointed out:

> My family has always been active with our culture. I have always known about my culture through my parents, grandparents, and relatives. The word "culture" means to me the knowledge of who I am, where I come from, and what are my traditions. Without my culture I would be no one. I wouldn't be able to tell you who I am. I try to be proud of my culture but when ignorant people start to say things that I don't like about Dominicans, I feel upset.

Similar feelings were expressed by Clemencia, who also described the uniqueness that had been imprinted on her identity by her family's cultural ties:

> My culture is very important to me because it signifies my identity and my individuality, it makes me feel that I am unique and that my family has different traditions from others. My culture is what makes me feel that we are not made out of the same mold and that we have certain qualities that distinguish us from the rest. If I were to forget this it would be as if I forget a part of my own identity.

Some participants, whose parents had chosen assimilation in American society, expressed a sense of loss, as in Yeiza's case:

> Cultural genocide has had a direct effect on me. My parents have done all they can to completely Americanize themselves. I feel as though they have tried to rob me of my history, culture, and very being. They had good intentions. They were just trying to help me fit in, fit in this American society.

Students who had been in the United States for 5 years or less and had completed up to the fifth grade in their country of origin explained that they had begun to appreciate their culture upon leaving their country and coming to the United States. Erickson described this kind of experience in the development of identity as a "necessary turning point, a crucial moment when development must move one way or another, marshaling resources of growth, recovery, and further differentiation" (1968, p. 16), Such was the case of Ana, who stated:

> I realized I belonged to my culture when I arrived to [sic] the United States. My life has changed because now that I know that I belong to this culture, I have learned to value many things that in this country go [sic] without being recognized. To me, culture signifies my roots, my traditions, and my morals. Culture is very important in my life because I act according to my roots and my morals. I have felt very ashamed when, on the news, the only thing they say about Colombia is the traffic of drugs.

A desire to learn more about her culture, as well as the ability to compare and contrast the differences between cultural groups, was evident in Clemencia's case. She seemed to be experiencing what Phinney & Tarver (1988) described as a stage of identity search:

> To be sincere, I knew what culture I belonged to before, but I realized its importance when I came to this country, so I wanted to learn more about it. For me now culture means what a group of people have in common. For example, in our Hispanic culture we have different foods, languages, and dances. It also means the difference that exists between ethnic groups. Our culture and the

culture of this country differ greatly in customs and traditions, which are manifestations of culture in itself.

Lorraine experienced a temporary dislodging of her previous view of the world (see Cross, 1978), as she encountered herself in a new environment that forced her to reinterpret her own view of her identity:

> I realized I belonged to a different culture when I left my country to come to the United States. Realizing what culture I belong to has made me appreciate it even more. The word culture means to me the origins and traditions of a person. My culture is of great importance in my life now. I think that one's culture must be preserved and one must be proud of what one is.

A similar situation was described by Alexia, who seemed to have achieved what Cross described as "internalization," a stage of identity which is characterized by "a calm, secure demeanor [where] ideological flexibility, psychological openness, and self-confidence...are evident" (1978, p. 18).

> I have always been aware of my Latin American heritage, but before, when I lived in my country, I did not appreciate it as much and took it for granted. Now that I live in the United States I am very proud of everything related to my culture and I do not regret being a Latina.

> My life has changed due to the fact that now I am prouder of my heritage and feel good when I speak about it, so that I can educate others and help them understand the Latino way of life. Now I appreciate more the cultural traditions of my country. To me, culture signifies my customs, my roots, my traditions, my way of life. Culture is a very important part of my life because it reflects my way of life and it is something I want to pass on to my children and grandchildren in the future.

The preservation of one's culture was a major concern of the participants. Sabrina recommended that we "teach each generation to be proud of its culture and...always they should keep their heads high." Clemencia echoed Sabrina's words: "What we can do is to transmit our traditions and customs to our children and grandchildren. In this way, our culture will never be forgotten." Lorraine concurred, saying: "In order to preserve our culture we must teach our children that our culture is important and that they should not let it die." Rodrigo suggested:

> To preserve our culture we have to practice our culture and not imitate other cultures, act like we belong to our culture not like the other people from other cultures act, learn more about our culture, and transfer it to our children. We must learn more about our culture and transfer it to our children so that, in the future, they know where their roots come from.

Alicia's words summarized the general feelings expressed by the participants about the role of culture in their personal lives:

> Culture.... It's my life. I believe culture is a big part of me: the traditions I keep are all part of my culture. It's important to me simply because it's part of my history and through it, I learn more about myself each day. Culture helps people find their identity, to know that they have something special about them, that there's something different about them. It all depends on their culture.

Alicia's comments lead to reflection on the role of schools in fostering cultural identity. If culture is such an important part of a child's life, why is it that educators fail to incorporate it within the school curriculum?

The discrepancy between what education provides for an individual whose language and culture are the same as those of the rest of the student body and those whose culture is different was described by Yeiza, who had seldom been exposed to her cultural heritage and language:

> The education I receive at this school is supposed to be important for me to advance in society. It helps me to identify myself as a capable and intelligent person, but it does not help me to identify with my culture and my roots.

Giroux states that students should "interrogate their inner histories and experiences...[and] understand how their own experiences are reinforced, contradicted, and suppressed as a result of the ideologies mediated in the material and intellectual practices that characterize daily classroom life" (1983, p. 150). Alexia's words provided an example of such a situation:

> In this school one can grow intellectually but not personally when it refers to the history, culture, and family of the student. The teachers and administrators don't have the time or the desire and wouldn't even consider...to appreciate the cultural contribution that the students can provide.

Many scholars have researched the interaction between school and families who come from diverse ethnic and linguistic backgrounds (Ada, 1988b; Bronfenbrenner, 1986; Cazden, Carrasco, Maldonado-Guzman & Erickson, 1985; Cochran & Dean, 1991; Delgado-Gaitan, 1992; Harry, 1992; Jordan & Au, 1981; Phillips, 1983; Siegel & Laosa, 1983; Soto, 1989, 1992; Ogbu, 1982; Trueba, 1989; and Wong Fillmore, 1990). In most cases, a cultural mismatch seems to exist between schools and families. Natalia's words exemplified a similar situation in terms of what her parents believed was the role of teachers and the reality she faced at school:

> Ever since I was little my parents told me that my teachers were people I could go [to] for advice and talk to if my mother or father were not there. The teachers were supposed to take my parents' place for part of the day. Having this in mind, I supposed that my teachers would recognize and appreciate my beliefs, background, and culture. Unfortunately, it is not like that at all.

The lack of incorporation of the students' culture in the classroom was of paramount concern to the participants. Carolina stated: "Unfortunately, some teachers are very ignorant and do not appreciate what we have to offer in order to learn about us in our classes." Alicia also addressed this issue, in terms of what the families of the students could contribute:

> The teachers at this school don't care about our culture. They do not incorporate culture in their classes. We have a lot to offer and most of this information comes from our parents, our families, but the teachers don't care about this.

Lorraine's words mentioned that the school's lack of appreciation of the students' culture made some of them want to assimilate in order to survive:

> This school does not focus on the importance of our culture. It does not try to help the Latino students learn who they are, and it does not try to learn from the students. This is why students forget their own culture to try and survive here. I think that's sad.

According to Giroux, "the notion that students come from different histories and embody different experiences, linguistic practices, cultures, and talents is strategically ignored" (1988, p. 125). Such a perspective addresses the need for teachers to acknowledge, respect, and value the culture of the students by giving them the opportunity to explore it within the classroom. Danny's words echoed similar feelings and also saw such an opportunity as a means to promote a "better understanding" among students:

> If my teachers realized the amount of information that each of us have, they would give us the time to express our feelings about our cultures, families, and personal histories. This would lead to a better understanding among students and would foster communication rather than separation between groups.

Some participants considered ignorance as the reason why teachers treated children of color differently, including Anita:

> It is due to ignorance that some of the teachers treat their students differently and make them suffer when they belong to a different culture or race, or when they speak a different language.... The teachers need to learn that they have to become involved with people of different backgrounds and should not mistreat them because they think that they are inferior.

Anita's words provided another insight into how students perceive teachers. She considered that it was due to ignorance, not malice, that teachers mistreat the students who belong to a different group. A plea for educators to change their perspectives and give children of color the respect they deserve as equal human beings was also stressed by her, as well as by other participants.

Language can be considered a means of expression and a vehicle for the transmission of culture. As such, it directly influences the development of ethnic identity and indelibly marks an individual's soul. It provides a frame of reference for future experiences, thus enhancing self-worth and self-esteem. The annihilation of a person's language is often the aim of a dominant group, which considers language a tool for the development of a hegemonic society and fears the existence and maintenance of other languages. The participants' descriptions often conveyed a sense of pride in their language, which they considered an integral part of their identity, and a feeling of contempt toward those who tried to silence them.

Most participants defined language as the expression of the self. In Carolina's words, "My language is the expression of who I am." According to Shor and Freire, "Language is also culture" (1987, p. 53), a point which was illustrated by Alexia:

> My language is a reflection of my history and my culture. Within any culture and language there are regionalisms. For example, in Spanish, people in different parts of Latin America have a different way of speaking and use different words that are not used in other parts of the Spanish-speaking world.... At school, I perfect my English and my Spanish.

Natalia addressed the duality existent within herself as a speaker of two languages, Spanish and English, and also the differences within the language itself:

> Language is an expression of me.... I am of Spanish descent, and speaking the language reflects that part of me. But in the Spanish language there are many different varieties. Each Spanish-speaking country adds various phrases, words, expressions that are special to that country.

The effort to promote "English only," often carried out by teachers and administrators, was of great concern to many of the participants, as stated by Alicia: "There are problems with teachers who don't believe that the students should be speaking Spanish in America, because they say that we are supposed to be speaking English only."

Many school officials continue to believe in the melting pot theory, which argues against multicultural diversity. This point was discussed by Ryan, who felt such efforts may lead to assimilation, and thus the annihilation of his own identity:

> Language, to me, is a part of my culture, a part of my heritage. It identifies me in a world that wants assimilation. I should be able to speak my own language in any place, any country because my language is a form of my expression in itself...but there are problems with discrimination, racism, and some teachers that only want you to speak English in America.

Madeline and Alexia recounted an incident that exemplified how teachers overtly attempted to force students to speak English instead of Spanish:

> We were walking up the staircase during change of classes and we were speaking in Spanish. A teacher came up to us and told us to either speak English or shut up. We felt really angry because she was trying to silence us by not letting us express ourselves in our own language.

Clemencia's words summarized the general feelings of most participants, that, by rejecting their language, culture, and home-based experiences, the school placed them in the periphery rather than at the center:

> It is hard not to feel rejected and marginalized because we speak a different language and belong to a different culture. We try to keep on thinking that we are not inferior, only different, but just as important in one way or another. Some people tell me not to speak Spanish because I am not in my country, but I don't pay attention because my language is a part of me and no one can make me hide it or feel ashamed of it.

Again the participants' comments reflected the deep sense of marginalization felt by children of color within the school system. They also stressed the struggle experienced by the students as they strived to maintain a sense of pride and dignity, yet were overtly and covertly made to feel inferior to the rest of the students.

Education can be seen as a liberatory learning process in which all individuals, regardless of class, race, gender, and ethnicity, become conscious of their ability to promote effective change for the betterment of society. Deconstructing preconceived notions that benefit only the dominant minority, liberatory education promotes the transformation of the self, thus creating opportunities for dialogic retrospection. Reflection plays an essential role in this process, since it provides an opportunity to look back, connect previous experiences to present realities, and construct meaning.

Describing what students consider alternatives to promote the emergence and legitimization of voice in the educational system is the central topic of this section. Most participants viewed education as a lifelong process that was not confined to attending specific institutions. This process involved the individual's desire to change internally, as well as maintain a balance and make connections between what is taught at home, outside school, and inside the school system. The participants struggled to build bridges between the three areas, but had a difficult time doing it. Lack of time to reflect seemed to be one of the major reasons why students experienced such difficulties.

According to Aronowitz and Giroux, "the school...had become the wish mechanism for Americans: that more citizens placed hope for their children in [the schools]...that it was up to the individual to perform well in the classroom in order to achieve liberation from manual labor" (1985, p. ix). Similar feelings were expressed by Alexia, who questioned the role of the school in relationship to life, and insisted that the responsibility for achieving success was up to her as an individual:

> The school offers to teach me different things about life...how to cope in different life situations, but it really doesn't. I am the one that makes the difference. I am the one that has to want to learn and the one that has to have the initiative to become a better person.

The difference between the education that the school provides and the education she receives at home was outlined by Clemencia, who expressed her belief that

> Even though there is some education that is learned through going to school, and that is used to get a career, develop the intellect, and analyze some situations, there is another type of education, which is the one from the home. This type of education helps us to distinguish right from wrong, and helps us solve daily life problems, which are things not taught at school.

A demand for changes in education was an underlying concern for many participants. Natalia added:

> If I had a chance, I would change a lot of the teaching staff, lower class sizes, and provide new materials because our classrooms are too overcrowded and many of our books are outdated. Among the staff, there are very few teachers who truly care about the welfare of their students. They don't give of themselves in teaching.... If you fail, they feel it's not their problem.

According to Clemencia and Alexia, teachers ought to look further and not limit themselves to automatically following the teacher's guide or the assigned textbook:

> Well, I wish education would not be so *automatizada*. The teachers have everything they need to teach in a teacher's guide book, even the tests, and they don't go any further than that. I believe the teachers should give of themselves and delve deeper [*profundizar*] in what is taught. Sometimes the book has a mistake, and when we tell the teacher he says he had not noticed it, and I think it is because teachers don't see any further than what they have to do (give homework and exams). I wish education would be less strict, more free, and then learning would be more interesting. (Clemencia)

> I would recommend that the teachers try to get to know their students and allow them to speak about their culture and the topics that are important to them. Also, I would ask the teachers not to teach straight from the textbook and to make the lessons less monotonous and more relevant to daily life. (Alexia)

Many of the participants expressed a need to develop a methodology based on student-teacher involvement, reflecting the kind of pedagogical approach that Walsh described, in which students are "actively engaged...in collective production, investigation, and interrogation" (1991a, p. 139). Ana's words make this perspective clear: "I would change the method in which most teachers teach and would make them get their students more involved with the subject that they teach." Rodrigo advocated "an increase in students' participation and more dialogue between students and teachers." Similar comments were made by Yeiza, who also called for a shift in the locus of learning from teacher-centered to student-centered:

> I would involve students in their own learning process and would make them participants of their own learning, rather than have the teacher do it all. The problem in classrooms is that when you try to express your ideas and what you might want to study or what you might want to do, a lot of times the teachers already have a schedule and they don't really care what you are interested in.

A concern about teachers' perceptions of students' abilities was expressed by Lorraine:

> I think that some teachers think that some of their students are not capable enough, while other students are capable of too much. That should change because we are all capable of learning, some of us learn in different ways and still try to please the teacher.

Pedagogical approaches that would address the real life needs of students, or what Gramsci described as "the truly active participation of the pupil in the school, which can only exist if the school is related to life" (1971, p. 73), were deemed essential by many of the participants. Damisela stated:

> Since medieval times a teacher has directed a lesson at the front of the room and lectured while some students have fallen asleep. There is a difference between traditional ways such as banking, where the teacher deposits information and you regurgitate feedback information, and problem posing, where students have the advantage of learning what is *really* needed for life. Critical thinking and expression are essential parts of it. It is impossible to *memorize* everything they give you, but it is much easier to remember when you have *learned* it.

Memorization of facts, dates, and general information was considered by many participants the most often used method of teaching. However, this method lacked time for reflection, thus echoing Shor and Freire: "Learning is not a memory Olympics. The idea is to make critical reflection...the fundamental activity...to avoid flying over...to reach the end...in such a way as to avoid knowing how learning relates to reality" (1987, p. 86). As a result, students seldom had an opportunity to make connections:

> In this school most of what we do is memorize. Many times we don't even know the reason why or how it relates to anything, only that we have to learn it. Sometimes I feel that to memorize, I don't need a teacher, only a book. Teachers should realize that we need the time to reflect and think why things happen and how they relate to our own lives. (Clemencia)

Clemencia's words echoed Freire's plea to reject memorization and incorporate a self-transforming approach to education:

> To acquire literacy is more than to psychologically and mechanically dominate reading and writing techniques. It is to dominate these techniques in terms of consciousness; to understand what one reads and to write what one understands; it is to communicate graphically. Acquiring literacy does not involve memorizing sentences, words, or syllables—lifeless objects unconnected to an existential universe—but rather an attitude of creation and re-creation, a self-transformation producing a stance of intervention in one's context. (Feire, 1973, p. 48)

Natalia compared teaching methods and advocated a problem-posing approach that would allow her opinions to be "heard and understood," thus giving her voice a space within the classroom:

> Using the banking method in class is like teaching a dog how to sit and beg, or teaching a parrot how to repeat what was said to it. But we are not dogs, nor are we parrots; we are human beings with the need to express feelings and the desire to be understood. Not every student can grasp the information given through the banking method, but everyone, in every race, has the desire to be heard and understood...and what better way could we voice our opinions other than in problem-posing.

A plea for using the problem-posing approach, at least once, was expressed by Yeiza and Danny, who felt that, if teachers tried it, they might see the value of it:

> My purpose for writing is not to discount the importance of the traditional, banking form of learning. It is to highlight the value of straying from the traditional approach, even if only once, to allow the way for a new form of learning called problem-posing education. Then you can decide for yourself and see if it helps your class like it has helped us. (Yeiza)

> It's a shame that other teachers don't use or put into effect the problem-posing approach in all their classes. They would find it hard to adapt to the new system at first, but the results are impressive. This method of asking, thinking, talking, and acting helps students learn how to deal with the pressures in school and at home better, and speak up for themselves so they can advance and let nobody get in their path. (Danny)

The advantages of using this approach were described in detail by Natalia, who felt that it had helped the group to attain unity, increase self-esteem, and respect other people:

> I think that sitting and discussing issues about our society using the problem-posing method gives us a feeling of unity. Although we may be of a different color, have different cultures, and speak a different language, it does not mean that we, the Latinos, are inferior to the rest of the society.... That is one of the many specific pointers that working as a group has provided for us. We believe in ourselves now for who we are, as well as respect the world around us.

According to Yeiza, using the problem-posing approach had led her to become "more aware of my culture, origins, customs, and people. It was a new experience that instilled a sense of pride in my heart, and that pride will never die." It also provided an opportunity for her to

> Learn more than just facts and figures.... I learned about people's feelings, emotions, and experiences.... All of a sudden, they were no longer just

statistics, but real persons with heart, soul, and permanent emotional scars of discrimination placed there by ignorant people.

Perhaps educators will heed the students' voices and attempt to approach education through the problem-posing method, thus giving students an opportunity to engage in dialogue, while allowing themselves to be taught by their students.

Reflection is an active process that provides an opportunity to look at past experiences and relate them to future action. It creates a space for discovering new realms within the self and unveiling previously unknown connections that exist between an individual's life in relationship to the lives of others. Often, educators believe that they are not able to provide the space for reflection due to the need to complete predetermined syllabi and objectives. Students are shortchanged in this process since they cannot take the initiative and propose that they need time to step back before going on to the next item.

The art of reflection was seen by most participants as the process of looking back or, as Maturana and Varela stated, "the process of knowing how we know…an act of turning back upon ourselves…the only chance we have to discover our blindness and to recognize that the certainties and knowledge of others are, respectively, as overwhelming and tenuous as our own" (1987, p. 24). Ryan and Natalia expressed the powerful impact that reflection had on their personal lives:

> Reflection means to think back on what you've done, and think how that something has helped you or hurt you, and basically, how it has affected you physically and emotionally. In my Spanish class my teacher always encourages us to reflect on everything we do. She actually encourages us to reflect before we do something, to think about how what we are doing affects someone else. (Ryan)

> Reflecting means looking back on everything…. By reflecting, you can learn from your mistakes and get a full understanding of what you have learned. Although in most classes we memorize the material and move on without even reflecting on what it was we've just learned, in my Spanish class reflecting is a big part of our class. (Natalia)

Carolina described how the four steps of questioning, reflecting, voicing, and acting, which are linked to Freire's "concientization" process, had helped her in making decisions:

> The process of reflection is a part of my education in one of my classes at this school because my Spanish teacher teaches us to reflect by using four steps: question, reflect, voice, and act. This method is very effective for me because it

helps me think about things I have never thought about before and to make appropriate decisions.

For some participants, the art of reflection had been stressed at home since childhood. Parents and relatives had often guided them to reflect on past experiences and to learn from them. However, such an opportunity was seldom present within school, where teachers seemed always to want to rush through the syllabus. Participants were eager to engage in reflection and would often welcome the opportunity to stop, think, and make connections. They overwhelmingly stressed the need to incorporate time to reflect in each class.

The four major themes uncovered here provide an insight into how students perceive their cultural and linguistic reality within the school system. They unveil the participants' yearning to have a voice, to be treated with respect and dignity, to have their culture and language brought to the center, and to be considered capable of participating in developing their own curriculum. As the themes unfold, a need to revamp pedagogical approaches is forever present. Deeply engrained in the participants' words is a firm belief that teachers need to find out who their students are, what needs they face, and how their real lives and experiences can be incorporated as part of the plan of studies.

Foremost in the participants' comments is a desire to have adults elicit and legitimize their voices within the classroom setting. A move in such a direction would contribute to an increase in self-esteem and would strengthen the students' belief in the democratic aspect of education. Students' perceptions on why their voices are silenced center mainly on issues of fear. Teachers and administrators seem to be afraid of what may happen if students are allowed to voice their concerns. Stereotypes of Latino students' attitudes toward school, as well as xenophobia and denial of reality, also play an important role in silencing and suppressing students' voices.

Students perceived that many teachers were afraid they might lose power if students were allowed to actively come to voice in the classroom. Most participants believed that power meant control. Teachers and administrators were often seen as the only individuals with any active power in the school. As a result, students complained about being "under" the teacher's power at most times. Acquiring knowledge was conceived as an ongoing process that was not confined to the school setting. It was clearly stressed that power and knowledge were intimately connected, and the more knowledge individuals had, the more power they could obtain.

An area that participants considered one of the most important was ethnic identity. Culture, language, and identity were braided as integral parts. Participants stressed how each one of them was woven throughout life, contributing to the development of self-esteem. The role of the family in the development or suppression of ethnic identity was of utmost importance, since children see parents and relatives as the sources or transmitters of culture and language. Likewise, the school was seen as a potentially important contributor, which could play a major role by incorporating the home-based linguistic and cultural experiences of the students but often chose not to do so.

The participants in this study considered education to be a learning process in need of major reforms. Foremost, the students advocated the development of new methodologies that would be centered on their realities. Often there was a distinct separation between what the school teaches and what students' lives are about, with no connection provided as a bridge. Students were concerned with the overuse of memorization, and the lack of time to reflect on the material that was being taught. Reflection was considered an extremely important activity that should be incorporated as a part of every lesson. Problem posing was portrayed as a viable alternative to aid in the emergence of voice, since it provided opportunities for students to actively engage in dialogue and reflection.

The themes uncovered through the dialogical process are extremely significant in light of what students stated. They illuminate areas that need to be considered when planning an effective approach to education. Also, they reveal ways in which pedagogy and education need to change in order to provide equal opportunities for all students. These comments and perspectives support concerns and issues previously discussed in the review of the literature. Thus, they reinforce the belief that students are experts who need to be included as an integral part of the educational movement if effective change is to take place.

The four major themes are deeply interconnected in a myriad of ways. The students' comments reveal that coming to voice leads to the acquisition of power, thereby disrupting traditional educational approaches that portray the teacher as the sole holder of power in the classroom. A similar situation occurs with knowledge, which is regarded by the participants as the key to power. Therefore, if students' voices are acknowledged in the classroom, the unequal distribution of power is shifted. At the same time, the locus of learning and creation of knowledge becomes a dialogical process in which teacher and students alike can be cocreators.

Culture and language are central to the development of ethnic identity, which is an expression of the inner self called voice. The teacher, as a holder of power and knowledge, often chooses what is presented to the students in the classroom. Students clamored for the incorporation of their own culture, language, and home-based experiences as part of the curriculum, which, according to them, should be centered on their personal realities. Again, a rupture from traditional approaches was deemed necessary in order to shift the learning locus from teacher to student centered. Education was described as a learning process that needed to incorporate reflection as an essential element. Using a problem-posing approach was considered important as a means to actively incorporate students in the decision-making process, allowing them to introduce their concerns and seek viable solutions to their problems.

The students' voices contribute greatly to answering the initial research questions posed in this study. They shed light on issues that are seldom considered important by proposers of educational reform. Above all, the students' comments force teachers and administrators to ask what is the reality lived by students in the classroom and how pedagogical approaches need to change if the challenge of democracy is to be addressed. The participants' perspectives shatter many preconceived pedagogical notions, which are still reinforced in teacher preparation programs, and call for drastic reforms in the field of education.

CHAPTER FIVE
Reflections for the Future

Included in this final chapter is a general summary of the study and theme interpretations as described in chapter 4. Conclusions and theoretical, practical, and policy issues are also discussed in light of the participants' comments. The recommendations for action and the researcher's personal reflections include suggestions for approaches that place Latino students' voices at the center rather than the periphery of the curriculum, thereby honoring their language, culture, and home-based experiences.

This study set out to examine, through the participants' voices, some of the factors that promote the silencing of voice in Latino high school students, submersing them in the culture of silence. It aimed to discover how students perceive their cultural and linguistic reality, as well as their family history and home experiences, within the educational system. The study also examined at what students consider to be viable alternatives for promoting educational reform, including what can be done to aid the emergence and legitimization of their voices.

The methodology, naturalistic in nature, was designed to actively engage the students themselves in the research process and, in this process, to promote personal and social change. It drew from the principles of participatory research, emancipatory/praxis-oriented research, and qualitative activist research and was based on the process of "conscientization." The participants were 18 Latino high school students, from a Spanish for Native Speakers program in Florida. Dialectical, open-ended, sequential interviews constituted the vehicle for communication among the participants and the researcher. The dialogues took place at "Eastern High School" (E.H.S.), in Traviss, Florida. A total of 7 topics were covered by each participant, totaling 140 dialogues for the whole group.

The participants' comments were clustered around four central issues, which provide an insight into the students' perceptions of their own realities and illuminate areas that students consider must be incorporated into the learning process. Furthermore, the participants' perspectives reveal ways in which pedagogy and education need to change in order to provide equal opportunities for all students, regardless of class, race, gender, and ethnicity. The four major themes are (1) voice: rupturing the structured silence; (2) power and knowledge: a direct connection; (3) ethnic identity and its relationship to culture and language; and (4) education as a learning process involving reflection.

The study covered a time in the lives of adolescents that is marked by a presupposed growth in history and maturation. The words, reflections, and perspectives that emanated from this particular group of students were relevant to their own lived experiences and to the environment and context in which they were spoken. Therefore, the information needs to be read as related to that life period of these students and cannot be generalized to represent the voices of all Latino youth. As such, the findings may or may not apply in other contexts, thereby pointing to the need for more research in order to reaffirm the grounding theory. The honesty and depth with which the students were willing to portray their reality and reflect upon its implications show young Latino students' ability and willingness to take a very responsible part in their education.

The significance of this study rests on (a) its ability to draw out, explore, and document how Latino students perceive their cultural and linguistic reality; (b) its presentation of curricular and methodological approaches and viable alternatives to promote the emergence and legitimization of students' voices; and (c) its insight into and revelation of the ways shared teacher/student experiences, language, and culture can shape and impact both classroom relations and the emergence of voice.

Accepting the premise that students' voices are an untapped and unexpectedly diverse fountain of thoughts and perspectives, this study aimed to provide a forum where students' voices could be elicited, heard, validated, and legitimized. As a result, students and teacher became cocreators of knowledge in their shared attempt to answer the following research questions:

1. What are some of the factors that lead to the silencing of voice in Latino high school students?
2. What happens when their voices emerge?

3. What do students perceive as their cultural and linguistic reality within the educational system?
4. What are some alternatives that can promote the emergence and legitimization of voice in the educational system?

The following section presents conclusions related to each research question.

Most participants shared a common belief in the need to express their voices and use them as a political tool to obtain power. However, most teachers and administrators usually thwarted their attempts. Among some of the causes that led to the silencing of students' voices was fear, as expressed by Guillermo's comments: "They [administrators and teachers] try to silence our voices, in some cases, for fear, fear of us exposing those who try to oppress our race, for fear that we say what we feel...They are afraid."

Teachers and administrators seemed to be afraid of the unknown, that is, what might happen if students were allowed to come to voice and express their inner feelings and thoughts. Yeiza summarized the participants' general feelings: "We are silenced because people are fearful of our ideas and the power we might obtain with our voices." At times, fear appears to be rooted in xenophobia. Students perceived that teachers tended to reject them because they were different from the rest of the school population. As Ryan expressed it: "I think they might be afraid of what they don't understand. What's not familiar to them, they ...treat it like garbage.... Until they try to understand other foreign...cultures, I don't think this problem will ever be resolved."

Racism and discrimination, as well as teachers' negative perceptions of Latino students, were often mentioned as causes for silencing students' voices. As expressed by Alexia: "they perceive Latinos as students that never do anything, except misbehave,...never get their work done and always disrespect teachers and...they think that we are all like that and...are not worth it." Similarly, authoritarianism and denial of reality played an important role. Alicia stated, "They want to avoid getting the truth. You know, finding out what's really going on behind closed doors. They want to keep it under cover."

Observing what happens when students' voices emerge in the classroom setting was a central part of this study. It entailed the creation of a safe haven where students felt a sense of freedom of expression. Creating a safe haven for expression encompassed developing mutual trust, reciprocity, and respect, and believing in the ability of students to construct knowledge. It also included the use of a problem-posing approach, where students were considered experts who could contribute to the learning process. Honoring their voices and providing an opportunity to freely express their feelings and thoughts, the researcher promoted the emergence of voice, as Ryan's comments showed:

> In this class, I have a voice. I am allowed to express my ideas and opinions. It's like a whole different world. A world where my voice matters, and my opinions really count, because there is a key, the key to unlock everyone's voice. Even though some people are afraid of this key, my teacher inspires us with her ways of teaching, she encourages us to unlock that voice and share it with the world.

As their voices emerged, students seemed to develop a feeling of security and positive self-esteem. This feeling permeated their actions inside as well as outside school, providing a sense of well-being and greater self-confidence. Foremost in their comments was a sense of powerlessness within the classroom setting. Often they described how teachers ruled their classes, leaving no space for students' personal expressions. Given the opportunity, the participants engaged in dialogue and explored issues of concern to their daily lives, such as power and knowledge.

Contrary to traditional beliefs, the participants in this study did not see the teacher as the *only* source of knowledge, but considered that they, also, were sources of knowledge. In addition, the participants believed that knowledge was actually based on experience and could be acquired throughout life, thus echoing Dewey's words: "The most important attitude that can be formed is that of desire to go on learning" (1938, p. 48). This belief may have arisen from the fact that the students had been engaged in nontraditional pedagogical approaches, such as the ones previously described in the review of the literature, for a period of at least a year before the study took place.

Among the approaches used in the author's classroom were the creation of books coauthored with parents or relatives (Ada, 1992); the use of socio-drama to produce videos and short stories (Walsh, 1991a); and the development and design of a curriculum based on the generative themes chosen by students (Shor, 1992). Incorporating such approaches into the curriculum contributed to balancing the unequal distribution of power in the classroom by placing the students as teachers and the teacher as student (Freire, 1970).

Students' perspectives on their cultural and linguistic reality within the educational system illuminated areas often overlooked. The participants constantly referred to culture and language as integral parts of their identity, considering both as major parts of their lives and intimately connected. Parents and family seem to play a crucial role in the fostering or suppression of cultural identity. Cultural identity seemed to play a pivotal role, often providing a frame of reference for thoughts and actions. The formation of identity was a crucial factor in the development of self-esteem and personal pride. Preserving their culture was a major concern for the participants, who insisted it should be transmitted from generation to generation as a means of individual and group identification.

According to the participants, the school could also play an important role in the development of cultural identity. Unfortunately, teachers and administrators often seemed to ignore the students' cultural, linguistic, and home-based experiences, relegating these experiences to the periphery and contributing to the marginalization of Latino students. Most teachers and administrators did not seem able to address the needs and concerns of Latino students and their families. The participants sensed that such an attitude was often rooted in ignorance, and it was in dire need of change. A "culture clash" (Garcia, 1994) between home and school was forever present, and participants were often caught in the middle.

The participants considered education essential for advancement in society. Revamping the educational system was considered necessary. This move would involve not just curriculum, texts, and physical facilities but, above all, methodological approaches to teaching, with problem posing being a possible alternative. The participants' voices advocated the removal of educational policies and pedagogical practices that traditionally rule public school classrooms, encoding power and marginalizing Latino students. They clamored for a move, within the school curriculum, that would rupture the structured silences imposed on their history, culture, and language.

Underlying the students' comments was a direct concern with the difference between what the school teaches and the realities of their lives. The participants' comments were centered on what their lives are like in the outside world. They often spoke of family, culture, and language as being of great importance to their lives, yet there never seemed to be a connection between what is taught at home and what is taught at school. Again the participants reiterated the need for an inclusive curriculum that would actively incorporate the perspectives of the students, the parents, and the community.

The participants considered education as a learning process that needed to incorporate reflection. Reflection was seen as a process of looking back on the past that encouraged learning from past experiences to take place. As Natalia said, reflection led a person to "a full understanding of what you have learned." Some participants had been taught to reflect by their parents since childhood. The four step method of questioning, reflecting, voicing, and acting was mentioned by a participant as helping her to think about things she had never thought about before and then to make appropriate decisions.

The review of the literature indicates that the education afforded to children of color is directly tied to class, gender, race, language, power, and socioeconomic factors. Among the most salient factors are the interaction between schools and families, covert and overt attempts to assimilate Latino students into mainstream American society, the imposition of a non-inclusive traditional curriculum that fails to acknowledge and honor the culture, language, and home-based experiences of people of color. Consequently, Latino children are made to believe that their history and culture do not exist in the school curriculum or in school life. As suggested by Giroux:

> The system operates to deny some individuals voice, and their awareness of their lack of voice convinces them either that they have none, or that they want no part of a system that seeks to silence them. Educational institutions, in particular, function to reproduce existing power relations by imposing definitions of knowledge that reaffirm the culture of the dominant society. (1983, p. 174)

Regardless of how desperately the students' voices need to be elicited, heard, and legitimized, little seems to be happening to induce educators and administrators to engage in dialogue with students. Such realizations are cause for reflection on the situation being faced by Latino students, who are often marginalized within the educational system by peers and teachers alike. Issues of power, mainly in the form of domination and oppression, seem to be at the root of the problem.

Many public schools seem to have become assimilation sites. In overt and covert ways, they tend to promote the silencing of voice in Latino high school students. Such places dehumanize children by severing them from their linguistic and cultural ties, thus contributing to the dismemberment of the community. Freire stated: "As the oppressor minority subordinates and dominates...it must divide it and keep it [the oppressed majority divided.... The minority cannot permit itself the luxury of tolerating the unification of the people, which would signify a...threat to their own hegemony" (1970, p. 137).

Giroux argued in the following terms for the need to incorporate the histories of children of color and their communities within the school system:

> By urging an attentiveness to the suppressed moments of history, critical theory points to the need to develop an equal sensitivity to certain aspects of culture. For example...women, Blacks, and others need to affirm their own histories through the use of language, a set of social relations, and body of knowledge that critically reconstructs and dignifies the cultural experiences that make up the tissue, texture, and history of their daily lives. (1983, p. 37)

Considering the oppressive conditions faced by children of color in the educational system, there is a need to create a more inclusive, less restrictive environment that can foster mutual respect and understanding among all members of the school community. Such an environment should include the students' language, culture, and home-based experiences as a central part of the curriculum. The incorporation of the lived histories of the communities of people of color seems to be an essential element that is presently lacking in the system. Pedagogical practices that encourage the construction of meaning and the generation of knowledge are also necessary in order to shift the locus of learning from teacher to student centered. However, two of the most important tasks still remaining for educators are "to help students identify the multiple forms of domination that restrict their possibilities and position their understanding...[and] to develop pedagogies that encourage students to take action toward transforming that which limits them" (Walsh, 1991a, p. 138).

The findings presented in this study offer an in-depth view of how students' perspectives can illuminate areas of research often unexplored, and how their perspectives can greatly contribute to promote more effective reforms in the field of education. Such findings are in agreement with much of the recent literature on students' voices (Nieto, 1994; Poplin & Weeres, 1992; Zanger, 1994; Walsh, 1996). They also expand previous findings in the area of ethnic identity as it relates to language and culture. It is in this area that they reflect the unique aspects of the cultural composition of the class studied. These findings are embedded in a particular context, and cannot be fully understood except in context.

The recommendations for action come from the participants and the researcher. The participants' words advocate action within the classroom. The researcher's recommendations are divided into two sections. The first section refers to action that can be taken by teachers in their classrooms. The second section addresses issues that can be implemented in teacher-training programs. Finally, there are recommendations for further research.

At the end of the study, the participants were asked what general recommendations for action they would give teachers in order to improve the conditions existing in school today. Resonant among the participants' concerns is the desire for a change in methodological approaches and pedagogical practices. The following quotations summarize their comments and suggestions and provide general guidelines for specific action within the classroom:

> My advice to teachers is to give students time to think and reflect about topics that connect the curriculum with their daily lives. Education should not be based on lectures and memorization, it should be based on topics that are typical of the lives of teenagers today (such as racism and discrimination). (Natalia)

Pablo's words summarized the general feelings expressed by the participants in reference to the establishment of a closer relationship between teachers and students, similar to the relationship Mercado described as caring as empowerment (1993):

> My recommendations to present and future teachers are that they become more involved in the personal lives of their students. I also recommend that they prepare activities that reflect what happens in the lives of their students. Many teachers never pay a lot of attention or make efforts in helping students cope with their personal lives. Such effort on the teacher's part leads to the establishment of a strong relationship between teacher and student, a relationship so strong that it never dies. (Pablo)

Alexia also addressed the need for teachers to get to know their students, as well as to allow them to contribute to the curriculum, by incorporating their cultures and lived realities:

> I would recommend to other teachers that they make an effort to get to know their students and to let them speak about their cultures and those things that are important to their lives. When a teacher tries to get to know her students

and to help them, the students grow emotionally and spiritually and the class, as a group, becomes more united. (Alexia)

The participants call for teachers to believe in the participatory nature of learning, in which students collectively engage in investigating, interrogating, and producing knowledge. The use of themes that are grounded in their lives as part of the curriculum is another important issue for the students. Foremost, the students want teachers to engage with them as individuals, to affirm them as human beings, and to allow for the establishment of personal relationships grounded in spiritual, emotional, and intellectual levels.

The following recommendations are based on the researcher's interpretations of her findings, as well as her experience as an educator, and her understanding of pedagogical practices that may elicit the emergence of students' voices.

1. Pedagogical practices should be reexamined in order to provide congruence with various styles of learning and multiple intelligences. Reflection should be incorporated as an essential component.
2. A more encompassing curriculum, not centered on Eurocentric perspectives, that acknowledges the histories, languages, cultures, and home-based experiences of people of color should be developed and implemented in order to provide a more accurate perspective of the world and to reveal the contributions of people of color to society.
3. Teachers and administrators should engage in dialogue with students of color in order to discover their realities and incorporate them within the plan of studies.
4. Teachers and administrators should participate in cultural awareness sessions that present the students' perspectives in order to address the needs and concerns of children of color.
5. Teacher-training programs (e.g., pre-service, public school in-service) should require a multicultural awareness course that emphasizes a change of attitude toward the histories, cultures, languages, and home-based experiences of people of color.
6. Teacher-training programs must incorporate methodological approaches that promote dialogue and reflection among participants in order to foster the emergence of voice in students. Prospective teachers who have experienced such approaches can

then incorporate them in their classrooms and explore their possibilities.

Perhaps the most important recommendation is to have similar studies conducted with different groups of students in different parts of the United States. It would be interesting to see how other students of color respond to the same issues, especially in the area of culture and language. For example, it is important to explore the perspectives of Native-American high school students, to see if they have gone through experiences similar to those of Latino students, within the educational system.

This study could also be carried out with a group of newly arrived non-native students.

The means of communication would not be English. It would be the students' native language. This study would explore their perspectives on their own language and culture as they begin attending school in the United States. A follow up could be done at the end of their first year to see if and how their perspectives have changed.

An interesting question to explore that remains unanswered by this study is: How do teachers see the emergence of students' voices in general, and specifically, as this pertains to students of color?

The findings of this study were primarily based on data generated using dialogic retrospection. The data-gathering process was incorporated as part of the plan of studies of the A.P. Spanish language class during the months before to the students took the A.P. exam. Other requirements had to be met; thus the time allotted for the dialogues had to be shortened. Due to the large number of participants and the time frame involved, only one dialogue per topic was conducted. The students and the researcher met on a daily basis as a class but dedicated only two periods a week to the dialogues. During this time, the participants carried out the dialogues, discussed general findings, pointed to similarities, and proceeded to transcribe the data. The researcher recommends that in future studies:

1. A minimum of three dialogues per topic, with the necessary sessions for reflection, should be conducted. An increase in the number of dialogues would allow more time to probe issues, generate more data, and produce higher levels of reflection.
2. If possible, the time frame should be increased from one semester to a full academic year. Participants would then have

more opportunities for interaction, reflection, and dialogue, and would not be limited by time constraints related to completion of course objectives and achievement of competencies.
3. Participants should be encouraged to keep a journal and write individual reflections after each session. The information thus gathered could then be incorporated into the study, adding to the contrastive analysis.
4. Participants should be responsible for transcribing their dialogues in class in order to foster the sense of ownership of the process.
5. An action component could be incorporated as part of the research plan, to provide participants with a venue for transforming their reality. This component could take the form of a video, booklet, or flyers directed to educators and administrators, which could provide insights and suggestions.
6. The research questions for this study were generated independently by the researcher and then shared with the participants. It might be more appropriate to have the students determine what topics and questions they wish to pursue. The participants and the researcher jointly developed the questions to guide the dialogue. This approach lent itself to a sense of ownership on the participants' side.
7. The research design of the study did not provide for individual sessions, due to the number of participants. If possible, the researcher should meet with each participant on an individual basis to further encourage the process of self-reflection.
8. The identification of participants for this study was done on a voluntary basis. All 18 members of the class chose to be involved, thus providing a large number of responses and an array of perspectives. If the number of participants could be limited to 8, a deeper level of reflection might be achieved.

Conducting this study afforded the researcher an opportunity to gain more knowledge and insight into the world of Latino high school students and their communities. The participants' voices opened a window to a particular world, often unexplored by educators, and far more complex than one can imagine. The themes identified and discussed present only a part of the findings. Emerging as a result of the researcher delving deeper into the analysis of and reflection on the process are other more profound and fundamental issues, such as the need to talk of love, trust, and hope at the core of the learning process. The need to recognize the nature of humanness as an ability to know and transform in order to create a more equal and just society is also evident, as is the need to incorporate the use of dialogue and reflection as pedagogical practices.

Frightening for the researcher is the realization that students and educators seem to exist in two separate school worlds that are totally apart and seldom come in contact with one another. The school world perceived by students does not coincide with the school world educators see. As a result, educators address issues that they consider important, without realizing where students' perspectives are centered and what their needs are. Perhaps the inclusion of dialogue between the groups would bring a better understanding of the situation.

Feelings of love, the inclusion of caring as empowerment, and the belief that all human beings are capable of creating knowledge are important aspects that also need to be incorporated in the learning process.

> Let me say, with the risk of appearing ridiculous, that the true revolutionary is guided by strong feelings of love. It is impossible to think of an authentic revolutionary without this quality. (Che Guevara, quoted in Gerassi, 1969, p. 398)

Such a process also demands true, long-term commitment and, as Walsh stated, "a willingness to love, to take chances, to remain present, and to be a part of a shared struggle" (1992, p. 86). Furthermore, and perhaps even more important, we need to realize that "[i]n such work, the distinctions between the personal, the professional, and the political are blurred. The relationships that emerge cannot be entered into lightly nor can one expect that when a project ends they can withdraw" (Walsh, 1992, p. 88).

REFERENCES

Ada, A. F. (1992). Parents and children as authors and protagonists: A critical pedagogy approach to home-school interaction. In *Reclaiming our voices: Transforming education for cultural democracy Part II, Readings for the 1992 Institute.* Ontario, CA: California Association for Bilingual Education.

Ada, A. F. (1990a). *A magical encounter: Spanish-language children's literature in the classroom.* Compton, CA: Santillana Publishing Company, Inc.

Ada, A. F. (1990b). *The educator as researcher: Principles and practice of participatory research.* Paper presented at the Annual Meeting of the National Association for Bilingual Education, Tucson, AZ.

Ada, A. F. (1988a). Creative reading: A relevant methodology for language minority children. In L. M. Malave (Ed.), *NABE '87. Theory, research and application: Selected papers.* Buffalo: State University of New York Press.

Ada, A. F. (1988b). The Pajaro Valley experience: Working with Spanish-speaking parents to develop children's reading and writing skills in the home through the use of children's literature. In T. Skuttnab-Kangas and J. Cummins (Eds.), *Minority education: From shame to struggle.* Clevedon, Eng.: Multilingual Matters.

Agramonte, I. (1991). *Las doctrinas educativas de Marti.* San Juan, Puerto Rico: Editorial de la Universidad de Puerto Rico.

American Association of University Women. (1992). *Shortchanging girls, shortchanging America: A call to action.* Washington, DC: AAUW Initiative for Educational Equity.

Amidon, B., & Flanders, N. A. (1963). *The role of the teacher in the classroom: A manual for understanding and improving teachers' classroom behavior.* Minneapolis, MN: Paul S. Amidon & Associates.

Anderson, G. L., & Irvine, P. (1993). Informing critical literacy with ethnography. In C. Lankshear & P. McLaren (Eds.), *Critical literacy: Policy, praxis, and the postmodern.* Albany, NY: State University of New York Press.

Andriola-Balderas, V. (1995). To be alive in struggle: One teacher's journey. In J. Frederickson, *Reclaiming our voices: Bilingual education, critical pedagogy and praxis.* Ontario, CA: California Association for Bilingual Education.

Anzaldua, G. (1987). *Borderlands/La frontera: The new mestiza.* San Francisco: Spinsters/Auntlute Press.

Apple, M. W., & King, N. (1977). *What do schools teach? Humanistic education.* Berkeley: McCutchan.

Aronowitz, S., & Giroux, H. (1991). *Postmodern education.* Minneapolis, Minnesota: University of Minnesota Press.

Aronowitz, S., & Giroux, H. (1985). *Education under siege.* London: Routledge & Kegan.

Auerbach, E., & Wallerstein, N. (1987). *ESL for action: Problem-posing at work.* Reading, MA: Addison-Wesley.

Baker, D. (1986). Sex differences in classroom interactions in secondary science. *Journal of Classroom Interaction 22,* 212–218.

Beekman, T. (1986). Stepping inside: On participant experience and bodily presence in the field. *Journal of Education, 168*(3), 43.

Belenky, M. F., Clinchy, B. M., Goldberger, N. R., & Tarule, J. M. (1986). *Women's ways of knowing.* Cambridge: Basic Books.

Bellack, A., Kliebard, H. M., Hyman, R. T., & Smith, Jr., F. L. (1966). *The language of the classroom.* New York: Teachers College Press.

Benson, J. K. (1983). A dialectical method for the study of organizations, In *Beyond method: Strategies for social research* (Ed.). G. Morgan. Beverly Hills, CA: Sage Publications.

Bernal, M. E., and Knight, G. P. (Eds.). (1993) *Ethnic identity.* New York: State University of New York Press.

Bogdan, R., & Biklen, S. (1982). *Qualitative research for education: An introduction to theory and methods.* Boston: Allyn and Bacon.

Bogdan, R., & Taylor, S. J. (1975). *Introduction to qualitative research methods.* New York: John Wiley & Sons.

Boyer, E. L. (1987). *College: The undergraduate experience in America.* New York: Harper & Row.

Boyer, E. L. (1983). *High school: A report on secondary education in America.* New York: Harper & Row.

Britzman, D. (1989). Who has the floor? Curriculum, teaching, and the English student teacher's struggle for voice. *Curriculum Inquiry, 19*(2), 143–162.

Bronfenbrenner, U. (1986). Ecology of the family as a context for human development: Research perspective. *Developmental Psychology, 22(6),* 732–742.

Brown, D., & Tandom, R. (1987). Interviews as catalysts. *Journal of Applied Psychology 63*(2), 197–205.

Brown, P. (1993). *Young mothers' voices: Reflections on abusive relationships; A feminist participatory research.* Unpublished dissertation, University of San Francisco.

Campbell, C. P., & Simpson, C. R. (1992). *The self-fulfilling prophesy: Implications for the training/learning process.*

Carnegie Corporation. (1986). *A nation prepared: Teachers for the 21st century.* New York: Carnegie Corporation.

Carnoy, M., & Levin,T. (1976). *The limits of educational reform.* New York: McKay.

Cazden, C., Carrasco, A., Maldonado-Guzman, A., & Erickson, F. (1985). The contribution of ethnographic research to bicultural, bilingual education. In J. E. Alatis & J. Staczek (Eds.), *Perspectives on bilingualism and bilingual education* (pp. 153–169). Washington, DC: Georgetown University Press.

Cecil, N. L. (1988). Black dialect and academic success: A study of teacher expectations. *Reading Improvement, 25(1,)* 34–38.

Cochran, M., & Dean, C. (1991). Home-school relations and the empowerment process. *The Elementary School Journal, 19*(3), 261–269.

Coladarci, T. (1986). Accuracy of teacher judgments of student response to standardized test items. *Journal of Educational Psychology, 78*(2), 141–146.

Colaizzi, P. F. (1978). Psychological research as the phenomenologist views it. *Existential-Phenomenological Alternatives in Psychology.* New York: Oxford University Press.

Coles, R. (1967). *Children of crisis: A study of courage and fear.* Boston: Little, Brown & Company.

Comstock, D. (1982). A method for critical research. In *Knowledge and values in social and educational research,* Eric Bredo and Walter Feinberg, Eds., pp. 370–390. Philadelphia: Temple University Press.

Cornbleth, C., & Korth, W. (1980). Teacher perceptions and teacher-student interaction in integrated classrooms. *Journal of Experimental Education 48,* Summer, 259–263.

Cross, W. (1978). The Thomas and Cross models of psychological nigrescence: A literature review. *Journal of Black Psychology, 4,* 13–31.

Crowl, T. K. (1971). White teachers' evaluation of oral responses given by White and Negro ninth grade males. *Dissertation Abstracts, 31,* 4540-A.

Darder, A. (1995). Bicultural identity and the development of voice. In J. Frederickson, *Reclaiming our voices: Bilingual education, critical pedagogy and praxis.* Ontario, CA: California Association for Bilingual Education.

Darder, A. (1992). California Association for Bilingual Education, Reclaiming Our Voices: Transforming Education for Cultural Democracy Part II, Readings for the 1992 Institute

Darder, A. (1991). *Culture and power in the classroom: A critical foundation for bicultural education.* New York: Bergin & Garvin.

Delgado-Gaitan, C. (1992). School matters in the Mexican-American home: Socializing children to education. *American Educational Research Journal, 29*(3), 495–513.

de Schutter, A., & Yopo, B. (1983). Desarrollo y perspectiva de la investigacion participativa. In G. Vejarano (Ed.), *La investigacion participativa en America Latina. Patzcuaro,* Michoacan, Mexico: CREFAL.

De Vos, G. A. (1993). A psycho cultural approach to ethnic interaction in contemporary research. In M. E. Bernal & G. P. Knight (Eds.), *Ethnic identity.* New York: State University of New York Press

Dewey, J. (1938). *Experience and education.* New York: Macmillan.

Diaz-Greenberg, R. (1995) Demonstrating a practical approach to critical pedagogy. *Clips, Journal of the California Literature Project, 2*(2), 4–7.

Diaz-Soto, L. (1993). Curriculum and instruction research: Native language for school success. *Bilingual Research Journal, 17*(1 & 2), Winter/Spring, 83–97.

Didham C. K. (1990). *Equal opportunity in the classroom: Making teachers aware.* Paper presented at the Annual Meeting of the Association of Teacher Educators, Las Vegas, NV, February 5–8.

Dreeben, R. (1968). *On what is learned in schools.* Reading, MA: Addison Wesley.
Dunn, L. (1987). *Bilingual Hispanic children on the U.S. mainland: A review of research of their cognitive, linguistic, and scholastic development.* Research monograph. Minnesota: American Guidance Service.
Dusek, J. B., & Joseph, G. (1983). The bases of teacher expectancies: A meta-analysis. *Journal of Educational Psychology, 75*(3), 327–346.
Erickson, E. (1968). *Identity: Youth in crisis.* New York: Norton.
Erickson, K. (1976). *Everything in its path.* New York: Simon & Schuster.
Fals-Borda, O., & Rahman, M. A. (1991). *Action and knowledge: Breaking the monopoly with participatory action research.* New York: Apex Press.
Faltis, C. (1990). Spanish for native speakers: Freirian and Vygotskian perspectives. *Foreign Language Annals, 23* (2), 117–126.
Fanon, F. (1967). *Black skins white masks.* (C. L. Markmann, Trans.). New York: Grove. (Original work published 1961).
Fine, M. (1987). Silencing in public schools. *Language Arts, 64,* February, 157–174.
Fine, M., & Vanderslice, V. (1992). Qualitative activist research: Reflections on methods and politics. In Bryant, F., et al., *Methodological issues in applied social psychology.* New York: Plenium.
Fitzgerald, J. (1993). Views on bilingualism in the United States: A selective historical review: *Bilingual Research Journal, Vol. 17* (1 & 2), Winter/Spring, 35–56.
Flanders, N. A. (1962). *Interaction analysis: A technique for quantifying teacher influence.* Paper presented at American Educational Research Association Meeting, Chicago, February.
Freire, P. (1985). *The politics of education: Culture, power and liberation.* Cambridge: Bergin & Garvey.
Freire, P. (1974). *Concientizacion: Teoria y practica de la liberacion.* Buenos Aires, Argentina: Ediciones Busqueda S.A.E.I.C.
Freire, P. (1973). *Education for critical consciousness.* New York: Continuum.
Freire, P. (1970). *Pedagogy of the oppressed.* New York: Continuum.
Freire, P., & Faundez, A. (1989). *Learning to question: A pedagogy of liberation.* New York: Continuum.

Freire, P., & Macedo, D. (1987). *Literacy: Reading the word and the world.* Westport, CT: Greenwood Bergin & Garvey.

Friedenberg, E. Z. (1959). *The vanishing adolescent.* Westport, CT: Greenwood.

Fueyo, J. M. (1988). Technical literacy versus critical literacy in adult basic education. *Journal of Education, 170*(1), 107–118.

Gadamer, H. G. (1975). *Truth and method.* New York: Seabury Press.

Gaines, M. L., & Dairs, M. (1990). *Accuracy of teacher prediction of elementary student achievement.* Paper presented at the Annual Meeting of the American Educational Research Association, Boston, April.

Galeano, E. H. (1973). *Open veins of Latin America.* New York: Monthly Review Press.

Gans, H. J. (1962). *The urban villagers.* New York: Free Press of Glencoe.

Garcia, E. (1994). *Understanding and meeting the challenge of student cultural diversity.* Boston: Houghton Mifflin Company.

Gardner, B. S., & Mueller, D. K. (1984). *Pygmalion revisited: Turning teachers into trainers. A faculty utilization guide for managers of training and development/continuing education.* Paper presented at the National Adult Education Conference (32nd), Louisville, KY, November 10.

Gaventa, J. (1988). Participatory research in North America. *Convergence 24*(2–3), 19–28.

Gerassi, J. (Ed.). (1969). *Venceremos—The speeches and writings of Che Guevara.* New York: Continuum.

Giroux, H. (1991). Introduction. In C. E. Walsh (Ed.), *Literacy as praxis: Culture, language, and pedagogy.* Trenton, New Jersey: Ablex Publishing Corporation.

Giroux, H. (1989). *Schooling and the struggle for public life.* Minneapolis: University of Minnesota Press.

Giroux, H. (1988). *Teachers as intellectuals.* New York: Bergin & Garvey

Giroux, H. (1983). *Theory and resistance in education: A pedagogy for the opposition.* New York: Bergin & Garvey.

Giroux, H., & Penna, A. (1979). Social education in the classroom: The dynamics of the hidden curriculum. *Theory and Research in Social Education, 7,* Spring 21–42.

Giroux, H., & Purple, D. (1982). *The hidden curriculum and moral education: Illusion or insight.* Berkeley: McCutchan.

Giroux, H., & Simon, R. (1988). Schooling, popular culture, and a pedagogy of possibility. *Journal of Education, 170,* November, 9–25.

Gitlin, A. D. (1990). Educative research, voice, and school change. *Harvard Educational Review 60*(4), November.

Glaser, B., & Strauss, A. (1967). *The discovery of grounded theory.* Chicago: Aldine.

Good, T. L. (1987). Two decades of research on teacher expectations: Findings and future directions. *Journal of Teacher Education,35,* 32–47.

Good, T. L., & Brophy, J. E. (1972), Behavioral expression of teacher attitudes. *Journal of Educational Psychology, 63,* 617–624.

Good, T. L., & Brophy, J. E. (1971). The self-fulfilling prophecy. *Today's Education,* April, 52–53.

Good, T. L., & Brophy, J. E. (1969), *Teachers' communication of differential expectations for children's classroom performance.* Report Series No. 25. Austin, TX: Research and Development Center for Teacher Education, University of Texas at Austin.

Goodlad, J. (1984). *A place called school: Prospects for the future.* New York: McGraw-Hill.

Goulet, D. (1992). Introduction. In P. Freire, *Education for critical consciousness* (p. x). New York: Continuum.

Gramsci, A. (1971). *Selections from prison notebooks.* New York: International Publications.

Hadley, S. Trevor. (1954) A school mark—Fact or fantasy? *Educational Administration and Supervision, 40,* 305–312.

Hall, B. (1993). Introduction. In Park, P. (Ed.), *Voices of change: Participatory research in the United States and Canada.* Westport, CT: Bergin & Garvey.

Hall, B. (1992). From margins to center? The development and purpose of participatory research. *The American Sociologist, 22* (4), Winter.

Hall, B. (1975). Participatory research: An approach for change. *Prospects 8*(2), 24–31.

Harry, B. (1992). An ethnographic study of cross-cultural communication with Puerto Rican–American families in the special education system. *America Educational Research Journal, 29*(3), 471–494.

Hoge, R. D., & Butcher, R. (1984). Analysis of teacher judgments of pupil achievement level. *Journal of Educational Psychology, 76*(5), 777–781.
Holmes Group, Inc. (1986*). Tomorrow's teachers. A report of the Holmes Group.* East Lansing, MI: Holmes Group, Inc.
Horton, M., & Freire, P. (1990). *We make the road by walking: Conversations on education and social change.* Philadelphia: Temple University Press.
Hough, J. B. (1967). *Training in the control for verbal teaching behavior—Theory and implications.* Paper presented at A.E.R.A. Convention, New York City.
Hughes, M. N. (1963). The Utah study of the assessment of teaching. In A. A. Bellack (Ed.), *Theory and research in teaching.* New York: Teachers College Press.
Jacob, E. (1992). Culture, context, and cognition. In M. D. Le Compte, W. L. Millroy, and J. Preissle (Eds.), *The qualitative research in education.* San Diego, CA: Academic Press, Inc.
Jackson, P. (1965). *Teacher-pupil communication: An observational study.* Paper read at A.E.R.A. Convention, February 1965.
Jackson, P. W. (1968). *Life in classrooms.* New York: Holt, Rinehart, & Winston.
Jarvis, P. (1987). *Adult learning in the social context.* London: Croom Helm.
Jordan, C., & Au, K. (1981). Teaching reading to Hawaiian children. Finding a culturally appropriate solution. In H. Trueba & G. P. Guthrie (Eds.), *Culture and the bilingual classroom.* Cambridge, MA: Newbury House.
Kenealy, P., Neil, F., & Shaw, W. (1988). Influences of children's physical attractiveness on teacher expectations. *Journal of Social Psychology, 128*(3), 373–383.
Kieffer, C. (1981). *Doing dialogic retrospection: Approaching empowerment through participating research.* Paper Presented at the International Meeting of the Society for Applied Anthropology, University of Edinburgh, April 5.
Kliebard, H. M. (1989). *Success and failure in educational reform: Are there historical lessons?* Occasional papers. The Holmes Group, Inc. East Lansing, MI: Michigan State University, 1989.

Kliebard, H. M. (1966). The observation of classroom behavior. In *The way teaching is*. Washington, DC: Association for Supervision and Curriculum Development and National Education Association.

Knight, G. P., Bernal, M. E., Cota, M. K., Garza, C. A., & Ocampo, K.A. (1993). Family socialization and Mexican American identity and behavior. In M. E. Bernal and G. P. Knight (Eds.), *Ethnic identity*. New York: State University of New York Press.

Kolb, D. A. (1984). *Experiential learning: Experience as the source of learning and development*. Englewood Cliffs, NJ: Prentice-Hall.

Kozol, J. (1991). *Savage inequalities*. New York: Crown Publishing.

Lankshear, C., & McLa. *Critical literary: Policy, praxis, and the postmodern*. Albany, NY: State University of New York Press.

Lather, P. (1991). *Getting smart: Feminist research and pedagogy with/in the postmodern*. New York: Routledge, Chapman, & Hall, Inc.

LeBoeuf, C. (1990). *The education experience of newly arrived immigrant high school students: A participatory reflection*. Unpublished dissertation, University of San Francisco.

Liebow, E. (1967). *Tally's corner*. Boston: Little, Brown & Company.

Lincoln, I. S., & Guba, E. G. (1985). *Naturalistic inquiry*. Newbury Park, CA: Sage Publications.

Maguire, P. (1987). *Doing participatory research: A feminist approach*. Amherst, MA: Center for International Education.

Marin, G. (1993) Influence of acculturation on familialism and self-identification among Hispanics. In M. E. Bernal and G. P. Knight (Eds.), *Ethnic identity*. New York: State University of New York Press.

Maturana, H., & Varela, F. (1987). *The tree of knowledge*. Boston: Shambhala Publications, Inc.

McCaleb, S. (1994). *Building communities of learners: A collaboration among teachers, students, families, and community*. New York: St. Martin's Press.

McLaren, P. (1989). *Life in schools: An introduction to critical pedagogy in the foundations of education*. New York: Longman.

McLaren, P., & Leonard, P. (1993). *Paulo Freire: A critical encounter*. New York: Routledge.

Medley, D. M., & Mitzel, H. F. (1963). Measuring classroom behavior by systematic observation. In N. L. Gage (Ed.), *Handbook of research in teaching*. Stamford, CN. Rand McNally.

Mercado, C. (1993). Caring as empowerment: School collaboration and community agency. *The Urban Review, 25* (1).

Merton, S. (1948). The self-fulfilling prophecy. *Antioch Review, 8*(2), 193–210.

Mezirow, J. (1981). A critical theory of adult learning and education. *Adult Education, 32,* 3–24.

National Commission on Excellence in Education. (1983). *A nation at risk: The imperative for educational reform.* Washington, DC: U.S. Department of Education.

Nieto, S. (1994). Lessons from students on creating a chance to dream. *Harvard Educational Review, 64*(4), Winter.

Ogbu, J. (1982). Cultural discontinuity and schooling. *Anthropology and Education Quarterly, 13,* 290–307.

Ortiz, F. I. (1988). Hispanic-American children's experiences in classrooms: A comparison between Hispanic and non-Hispanic children. In L. Weis (Ed.), *Class, race, and gender in American education* (pp. 63–86). Albany: State University of New York Press.

Palmer, P. J. (1983). *To know as we are known: A spirituality of education.* San Francisco: Harper & Row.

Park, P. (1993). *Voices of change: Participatory research in the United States and Canada.* Westport, CT: Bergin & Garvey.

Parsons, Talcott. (1959). The school class as a social system: Some of its functions in American society. *Harvard Educational Review, 29*(4), Fall.

Passow, A. H. (1984). Tackling the reform reports of the 1980s. *Phi Delta Kappan, 65*(10), 674–683.

Patriarca, L. A., & Kragt, D. M. (1986). Teacher expectations and student achievement: The ghost of Christmas future. *American Review,* May/June, 48–50.

Patton, M. Q. (1987). *How to use qualitative methods in evaluation.* Newbury Park, CA: Sage Publications.

Paz, O. (1962). *The labyrinth of the solitude: Life and thought in Mexico.* (L. Kemp, Trans.). New York: Grove. (Original work published 1950).

Phillips, S. (1983). *The invisible culture.* New York: Longman.

Phinney, J. I., & Tarver, S. (1988). Ethnic identity search and commitment in black and white eighth graders. *Journal of Early Adolescence, 8,* 265–277.

Poplin, M. (1993). Making our whole-language bilingual classroom also liberatory. In Villamil-J. Tinajero and A. Ada (Eds.) *The power of two languages: Literacy and biliteracy for Spanish-speaking students.* New York: Macmillan/McGraw-Hill School Publishing Company.

Poplin, M., & Weeres, J. (1992). *Voices from the inside: A report on schooling from inside the classroom. Part one: Naming the problem.* Institute for Education in Transformation at Claremont Graduate School.

Poplin, M. S. (1991a). *A practical theory of teaching and learning: The view from inside the transformative classroom: Contributions of constructivism.* Unpublished manuscript, Claremont Graduate School, Claremont, CA.

Poplin, M. S. (1991b). *A practical theory of teaching and learning: A view from inside the transformative classroom: Lessons from a pedagogy of the feminine.* Unpublished manuscript, Claremont Graduate School, Claremont, CA.

Poplin, M. S. (1991c). *A practical theory of teaching and learning: The view from inside the transformative classroom: Contributions of critical pedagogy.* Unpublished manuscript, Claremont Graduate School, Claremont, CA.

Purple, D. E. (1989). *The moral and spiritual crisis in American schools.* Evanston, IL: Northwestern University Press.

Rahman, M. A. (1991). The theoretical standpoint of PAR. In O. Fals-Borda, & M. A. Rahman (Eds.), *Action and knowledge: Breaking the monopoly with participatory action research.* New York: Apex Press.

Ramirez, J. D. (1991). Final report: Longitudinal study of structured English immersion strategy, early-exit and late-exit transitional bilingual education programs for language-minority children. (Contract No. 300–87–0156). Washington, DC: U.S. Department of Education, Office of Bilingual Education.

Reason, P., & Rowan, J. (1981). Issues of validity in new paradigm research. In Reason & Rowan (Eds.), *Human inquiry* (pp. 239–253). New York: John Wiley.

Rist, R. C. (1970) Student social class and teacher expectations: The self-fulfilling prophecy in ghetto education. *Harvard Educational Review, 40,* August, 411–451.

Rogers, C. (1959). Significant learning: In therapy and education. *Educational Leadership*, 232–242.
Rosenthal, R. (1991). Teacher expectancy effects: A brief update 25 years after the Pygmalion experiment. *Journal of Research in Education, 1,* Spring.
Rosenthal, R., and Jacobson, L. (1968). *Pygmalion in the classroom.* New York: Holt, Rinehart, & Winston.
Rubovitz, P. C., & Maehr, M. L. (1973). Pygmalion black and white. *Journal of Personality and Social Psychology, 24,* 210–218.
Sardello, R. J. (1971). A reciprocal participation model of experimentation. *Duquesne studies in phenomenological psychology volume I.* Pittsburgh: Duquesne University Press.
Seidman, I. E. (1991). *Interviewing as qualitative research: A guide for researchers in education and the social sciences.* New York: Teachers College Press.
Shaw, C. (1993). *Quench not the spirit.* Unpublished dissertation, University of San Francisco.
Shor, I. (1992). *Empowering education.* Chicago: University of Chicago Press.
Shor, I., & Freire, P. (1987). *A pedagogy for liberation: Dialogues on transforming education.* Westport, CT: Greenwood, Bergin-Garvey.
Siegel, I., & Laosa, L. (Eds.). (1983). *Changing families.* New York: Plenum.
Silberman, C. E. (1970). *Crisis in the classroom: The remaking of American education.* New York: Vintage.
Sirotnik, K. (1981). *What you see is what you get: A summary of observations in over 1000 elementary & secondary classrooms. A study of schooling in the United States.* (Tech. Rep. No. 29). Los Angeles: UCLA Graduate School of Education.
Sizer, T. (1992). *Horace's school.* New York: Houghton Mifflin Company.
Sizer, T. (1984). *Horace's compromise: The dilemma of the American high school.* New York: Houghton Mifflin Company.
Smey-Richman, B. (1989). *Teacher expectations and low-achieving students.* Philadelphia: Research for Better Schools.
Soto, L. D. (1992). *Bilingual families as educators of young children.* Research funded by the Spencer foundation.

Soto, L. D. (1989). The relationship between the home environment and the motivational orientation of higher and lower achieving Puerto Rican children. *Educational Research Quarterly, 13*(1), 22–36.

Spradley, J. (1979). *The ethnographic interview.* New York: Holt, Rinehart, & Winston.

Thorndike, Robert L. (1969) *Teachers College Record, 70* (8) May.

Trueba, H. T. (1989). *Raising silent voices: Educating the linguistic minorities for the 21st century.* New York: Newbury House.

Trueba, H. T. (1987). *Success or failure: Learning and the language minority student.* Cambridge, MA: Newbury House.

U.S. Commission on Civil Rights. (1973). *Report II: Mexican American education study.* Washington, DC: U.S. Government Printing Office.

U.S. Commission on Civil Rights. (1973). *Teachers and students: Differences in teacher interaction with Mexican American and Anglo students.* Report V: Mexican American Education Study. Washington, DC: U.S. Government Printing Office.

Vallance, E. (1973/1974). Hiding the hidden curriculum: An interpretation of the language of justification in nineteenth-century education reform. *Curriculum Theory Network, 4*(1).

Vio Grossi, F. (1981). Socio-political implications of participatory research. *Convergence, 14*(3).

Waggoner, D. (1993). The growth of multilingualism and the need for bilingual education: What do we know so far? *Bilingual Research Journal, 17* (1 & 2), Winter/Spring, 1–12.

Walsh, C. E. (1996). Making a difference: Social vision, pedagogy, and real life. In Walsh, C. E. (Ed.), *Education reform and social change: Multicultural voices, struggles, and visions.* Hillsdale, NJ: Lawrence Erlbaum.

Walsh, C. E. (1994). Engaging students in their own learning: Literacy, language, and knowledge production with Latino adolescents. In Spencer, D. (Ed.), *Adult biliteracy in the United States.* Washington, DC: Center for Applied Linguistics and Delta Systems.

Walsh, C. E. (1993). Becoming critical: Rethinking literacy, language, and teaching. In Villamil-J. Tinajero and A. Ada (Eds.), *The power of two languages: Literacy and biliteracy for Spanish-speaking students.* New York: Macmillan/McGraw-Hill School Publishing Company.

Walsh, C. E. (1992). Lecture given a the University of San Francisco School of Education, March 19.

Walsh, C. E. (1991a). *Pedagogy and the struggle for voice.* New York: Bergin & Garvey.
Walsh, C. E. (1991b). *Literacy as praxis: Culture, language, and pedagogy.* Trenton, New Jersey: Ablex Publishing Corporation.
Weber, R. (1991). Linguistic diversity and reading in American society. In R. Barr, M. L. Kamil, P. Mosenthal, & P. D. Pearson (Eds.), *Handbook of reading research, 2,* 97–119. New York: Longman.
Weinsheimer, J. (1985). *Gadamer's hermeneutics: A reading of truth and method.* New Haven, CT: Yale University Press.
Weis, L., & Fine, M. (1993). *Beyond silenced voices: Class, race, and gender in United States schools.* New York: State University of New York Press.
Westkott, M. (1977). Conservative method. *Philosophy of Social Sciences, 7,* 67–76.
Williams, J. H., & Muehl, S. (1978). Relations among student and teacher perceptions of behavior. *Journal of Negro Education, 47,* 328–336.
Wilson-Burkett, T. (1989). *What makes learning meaningful?* Paper presented at the Annual Meeting of the American Association for Adult and Continuing Education (Atlantic City, NJ, October 4).
Wong Fillmore, L. (1990). *Latino families and the schools.* California Perspectives, 1. San Francisco, CA.
Wolcott, H. F. (1990). *Writing up qualitative research.* Newbury Park: Sage Publications
Wu, R. (1990). *Experiences and reflections of Chinese immigrant youth: Implications for education. A participatory research.* Unpublished dissertation, University of San Francisco.
Zanger, V. V. (1994). Not joined in: The social context of English literacy development for Hispanic youth. In B. Ferdman, R. M. Weber, and A. G. Ramirez (Eds.), *Literacy across languages and cultures.* New York: State University of New York Press.

INDEX

A

Ada, A. F., 2, 3, 5, 29, 57
Agramonte, I., 15, 16
American Association of University Women, 11
Amidon, B., & Flanders, N. A., 9, 11
Anderson, G. L., & Irvine, P., 39
Andriola-Balderas, V., 29
Apple, M. W., & King, N., 5, 13
Aronowitz, S., & Giroux, H., 3, 5, 72
Auerbach, E., & Wallerstein, N., 5, 26

B

Baker, D., 11
Beekman, T., 41
Belenky, M. F., 41
Bellack, A., Kliebard, H. M., Hyman, R. T., & Smith, Jr., F. L., 11
Bernal, M. E., and Knight, G. P., 65
Bogdan, R., & Biklen, S., 41–42
Bogdan, R., & Taylor, S. J., 44
Boyer, E. L., 1, 10
Britzman, D., 4
Bronfenbrenner, U., 2, 68
Brown, D., & Tandom, R., 37
Brown, P., 5

C

Campbell, C. P., & Simpson, C. R., 12
Carnegie Corporation, 10
Carnoy, M., & Levin, T. 13

Cazden, C., Carrasco, A., Maldonado-Guzman, A., & Erickson, F., 2, 68
Cecil, N. L., 11
Cochran, M., & Dean, C., 2, 68
Coladarci, T., 12
Colaizzi, P. F., 39
Comstock, D., 42
Cornbleth, C., & Korth, W., 11, 12
Cross, W., 67
Crowl, T. K., 11

D

Darder, A., 1, 3, 5, 9, 12, 17, 28–29, 33–35
Delgado-Gaitan, C., 36
de Schutter, A., & Yopo, B., 37–38
De Vos, G. A., 63
Dewey, J., 27, 84
Diaz-Greenberg, R., 29
Diaz-Soto, L., 2
Didham C. K., 12
Dreeben, R., 13
Dunn, L., 2
Dusek, J. B., & Joseph, G., 11

E

Erickson, E., 66

F

Fals-Borda, O., & Rahman, M. A., 37, 39
Faltis, C., 16, 26

Fanon, F., 3
Fine, M., 5, 56
Fine, M., & Vanderslice, V., 8, 37, 39–41
Fitzgerald, J., 2
Flanders, N. A., 11
Freire, P., 1, 4–9, 14–16, 25–30, 32, 34, 38, 61, 63, 74, 84, 86
Freire, P., & Faundez, A., 28
Freire, P., & Macedo, D., 28, 63
Fueyo, J. M., 2

G

Gadamer, H. G., 15, 41
Gaines, M. L., & Dairs, M., 11
Galeano, E. H., 15
Garcia, E., 85
Gardner, B. S., & Mueller, D. K., 12
Gaventa, J., 37–38
Gerassi, J., 92
Giroux, H., 5, 7, 12–13, 17, 28, 31, 35, 56, 64, 68–69, 86–87
Giroux, H., & Penna, A., 13
Giroux, H., & Simon, R., 10
Gitlin, A. D., 13
Glaser, B., & Strauss, A., 40
Good, T. L., 11
Good, T. L., & Brophy, J. E., 12
Goodlad, J., 1, 10, 14–15, 59
Goulet, D., 4
Gramsci, A., 8, 74

H

Hadley, S. Trevor., 12
Hall, B., 37, 39
Harry, B., 2, 68
Hoge, R. D., & Butcher, R., 12
Holmes Group, Inc., 10
Horton, M., & Freire, P., 15
Hough, J. B., 11
Hughes, M. N., 11

J

Jackson, P., 11
Jackson, P. W., 7, 9, 12–13
Jarvis, P., 27
Jordan, C., & Au, K., 2, 68

K

Kenealy, P., Neil, F., & Shaw, W., 11
Kieffer, C., 39, 44
Kliebard, H. M., 9, 11, 16
Knight, G. P., Bernal, M. E., Cota, M. K., Garza, C. A., & Ocampo, K. A., 65
Kolb, D. A., 27
Kozol, J., 1

L

Lather, P., 37–40
LeBoeuf, C., 5
Lincoln, I. S., & Guba, E. G., 41–42, 44

M

Marin, G., 65
Maturana, H., & Varela, F., 76
McCaleb, S., 29
McLaren, P., 1, 5, 17, 28, 56, 64
McLaren, P., & Leonard, P., 64
Medley, D. M., & Mitzel, H. F., 9, 11
Mercado, C., 5, 88
Merton, S. 12
Mezirow, J., 27

N

National Commission on Excellence in Education, 9
Nieto, S., 5, 17, 21–24, 35, 59, 87

O

Ogbu, J., 2, 68
Ortiz, F. I., 11

P

Palmer, P. J., 13
Park, P., 28, 37, 39–40, 42
Parsons, Talcott, 13
Passow, A. H., 10
Patriarca, L. A., & Kragt, D. M., 12
Patton, M. Q., 42
Paz, O., 3
Phillips, S., 2, 68
Phinney, J. I., 66
Poplin, M., 5, 29
Poplin, M., & Weeres, J., 1, 5, 17–24, 35, 59, 87
Poplin, M. S., 1, 5, 10, 15

R

Rahman, M. A., 37, 39
Ramirez, J. D., 14
Reason, P., & Rowan, J., 37–38
Rist, R. C., 12
Rogers, C., 27–28
Rosenthal, R., 12
Rosenthal, R., and Jacobson, L., 12
Rubovitz, P. C., & Maehr, M. L., 12

S

Sardello, R. J., 39
Seidman, I. E., 44
Shaw, C., 5, 11
Shor, I., 4–5, 14–17, 25–26, 28–29, 32–33, 84
Shor, I., & Freire, P., 1, 9, 15, 37, 56, 70, 74
Siegel, I., & Laosa, L., 2, 68

Silberman, C. E., 1, 10, 12, 14
Sirotnik, K., 14
Sizer, T., 1, 14
Smey-Richman, B., 11
Soto, L. D., 2, 68
Spradley, J., 44

T

Thorndike, Robert L., 12
Trueba, H. T., 2, 68

U

U.S. Commission on Civil Rights, 11

V

Vallance, E., 13
Vio Grossi, F., 7, 37–38

W

Waggoner, D., 2
Walsh, C. E., 1–2, 5, 7–9, 15–17, 23–25, 28–29, 31–32, 35, 56–57, 59, 73, 84, 87, 92
Weber, R., 47
Weinsheimer, J., 41
Weis, L., & Fine, M., 1, 6, 9–10
Westkott, M., 38
Williams, J. H., & Muehl, S., 11
Wilson-Burkett, T., 27–28
Wong Fillmore, L., 2, 68
Wolcott, H. F., 44
Wu, R., 5

Z

Zanger, V. V., 5, 20–21, 23–24, 35, 59, 8

Studies in the Postmodern Theory of Education

General Editors
Joe L. Kincheloe & Shirley R. Steinberg

Counterpoints publishes the most compelling and imaginative books being written in education today. Grounded on the theoretical advances in criticism, feminism, and postmodernism in the last two decades of the twentieth century, Counterpoints engages the meaning of these innovations in various forms of educational expression. Committed to the proposition that theoretical literature should be accessible to a variety of audiences, the series insists that its authors avoid esoteric and jargonistic languages that transform educational scholarship into an elite discourse for the initiated. Scholarly work matters only to the degree it affects consciousness and practice at multiple sites. Counterpoints' editorial policy is based on these principles and the ability of scholars to break new ground, to open new conversations, to go where educators have never gone before.

For additional information about this series or for the submission of manuscripts, please contact:
    Joe L. Kincheloe & Shirley R. Steinberg
    c/o Peter Lang Publishing, Inc.
    275 Seventh Avenue, 28th floor
    New York, New York 10001

To order other books in this series, please contact our Customer Service Department:
    (800) 770-LANG (within the U.S.)
    (212) 647-7706 (outside the U.S.)
    (212) 647-7707 FAX

Or browse online by series:
    www.peterlangusa.com